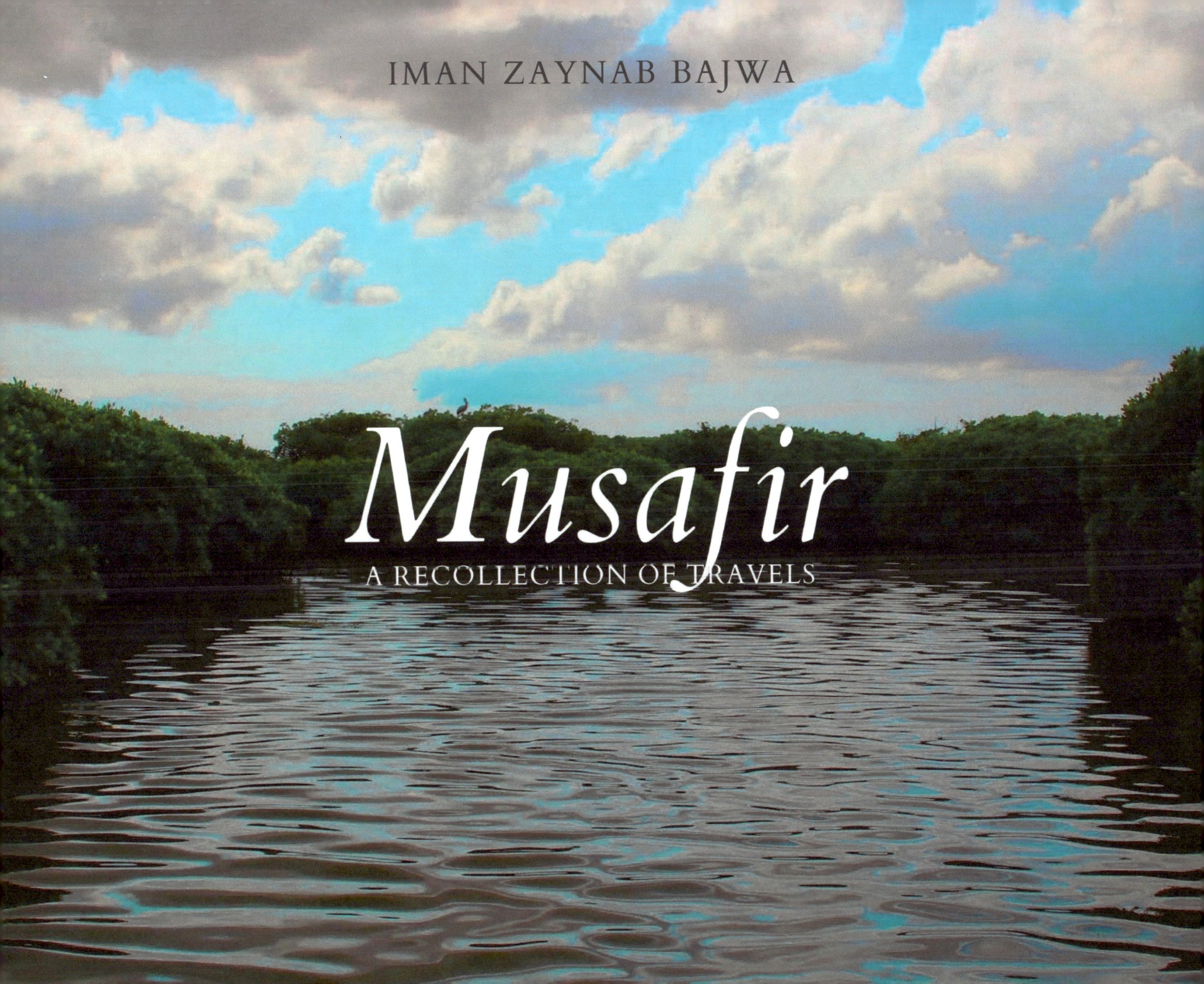

IMAN ZAYNAB BAJWA

Musafir
A RECOLLECTION OF TRAVELS

IMAN ZAYNAB BAJWA

Musafir
A RECOLLECTION OF TRAVELS

Shaherazad Shelves

To My Parents,
who've given me everything
so I can be where I am today

To Winter,
for being there for me
when no one else was

What is material possession, but a silencing of our souls.
A condemnation of our hearts, that yearn for actual gold.
What we truly seek, is not something that we can hide and keep.
It is a light that must be shared, a hope that must be spread. A love that must be taught, and justice for those who have fought.
We may pile up our gems and stones, hide in our homes of bones, but we can not run from our holes.
We are a sinking people.
Ready to be lost into time, unknown.

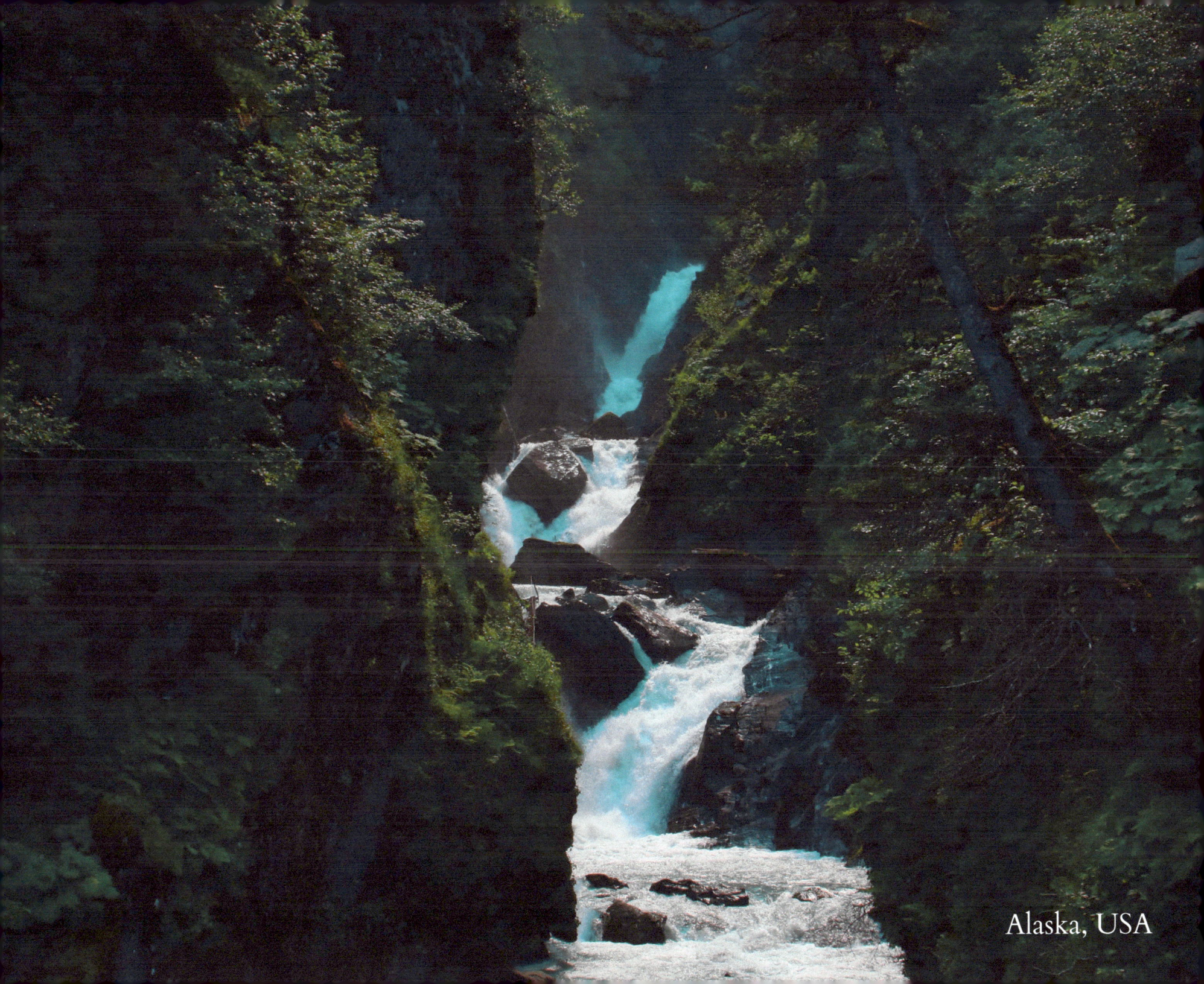

Alaska, USA

I feel the sea beneath my skin.
Vast and angry, depthless and ferocious.
It spares none, not even my wrecked soul, from the viciousness it holds.
Waves crashing, it destroys all that it seeks.

It runs red, the color of my rage, with the blood it has shed.
Masking what used to be obvious.
Trapping those unfortunate to replenish the evil lying within.
Lying deep beyond sight, yet close enough to bite.

All those who dare, pay the fare.
All those watching, learn their share.
Spread the warning, my little birds, of those who dared to cross me.
Of those who thought themselves worthy.
For as they fall, I rise.
And with me, I bring a new tide.

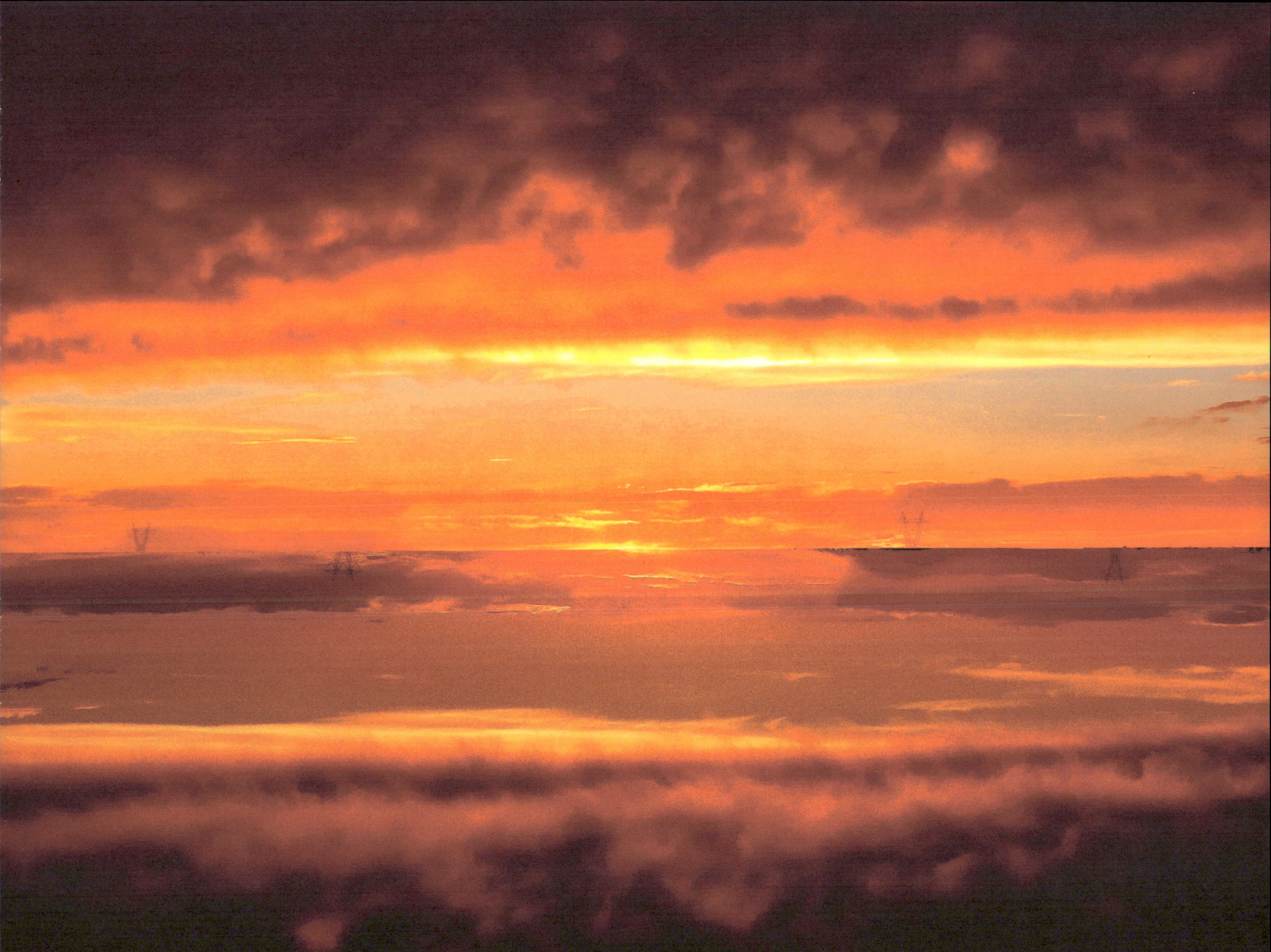

You ask us why we're so upset
As if we don't have a reason to be
Growing up in a world that's not working for us
All this pain and injustice, right in front of us

The internet; our savior, our downfall
A blessing and a curse
The light at the end of the tunnel and the darkness that plagues it
Everyday, bodies fall
Images pile up onto our broken hearts
Fingers struggling to pull down the refresh bar

A digital generation, a world so connected
Children so broken, angry and helpless
Few understand what it is like
To feel as if it is either our responsibility's might that will stop this plight
Or believe it to be futile and give up what's right

Punished for crimes we do not commit
Associated with us by the color of our skin
Marginalized and targeted, disunited and hateful
Our civilization crumbling before us as we refuse to watch
Lost in what they want us to be focused on
Not realizing the truth of it all

And yet, you ask us why we are upset
As if we don't have a reason to be?

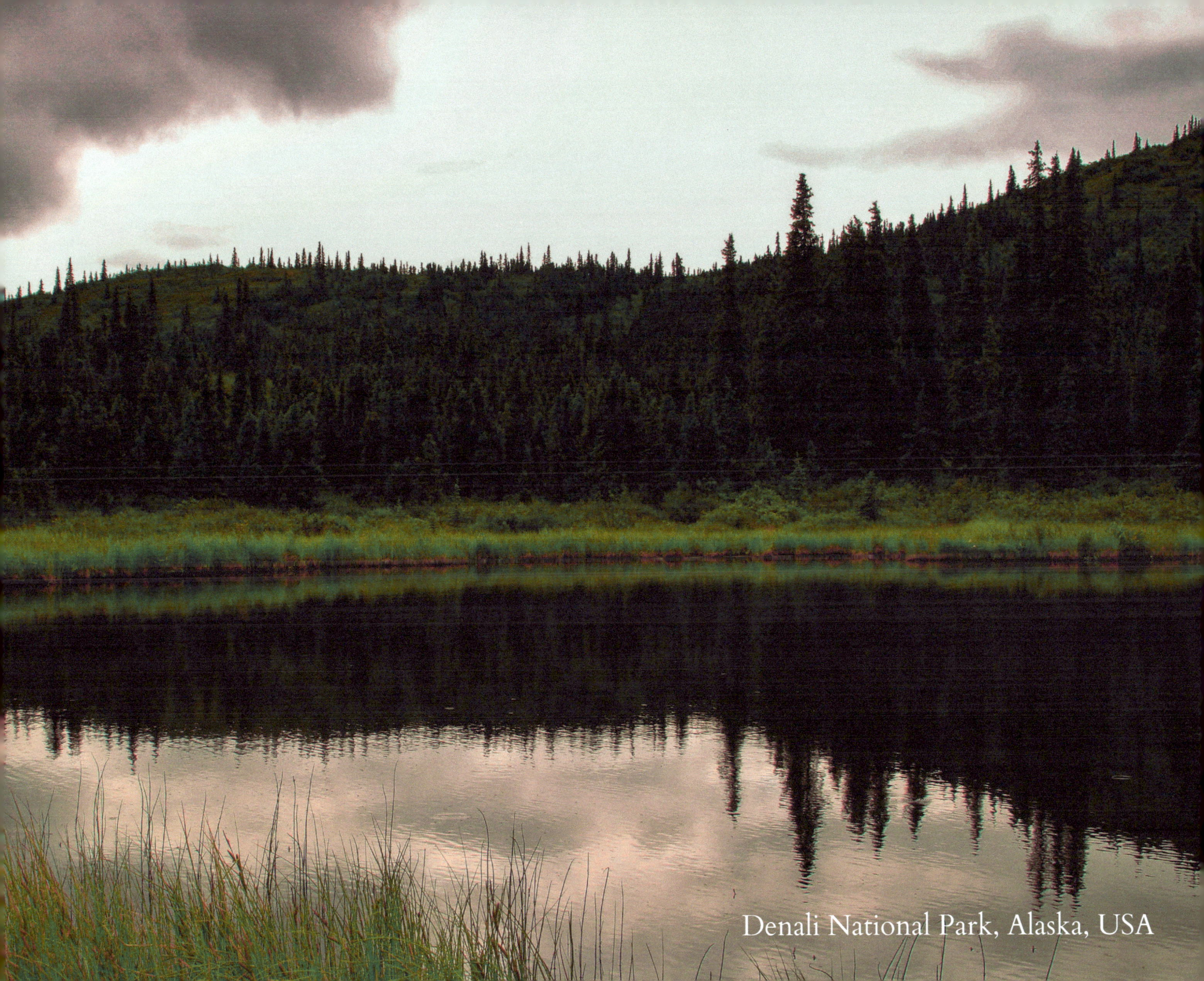

Denali National Park, Alaska, USA

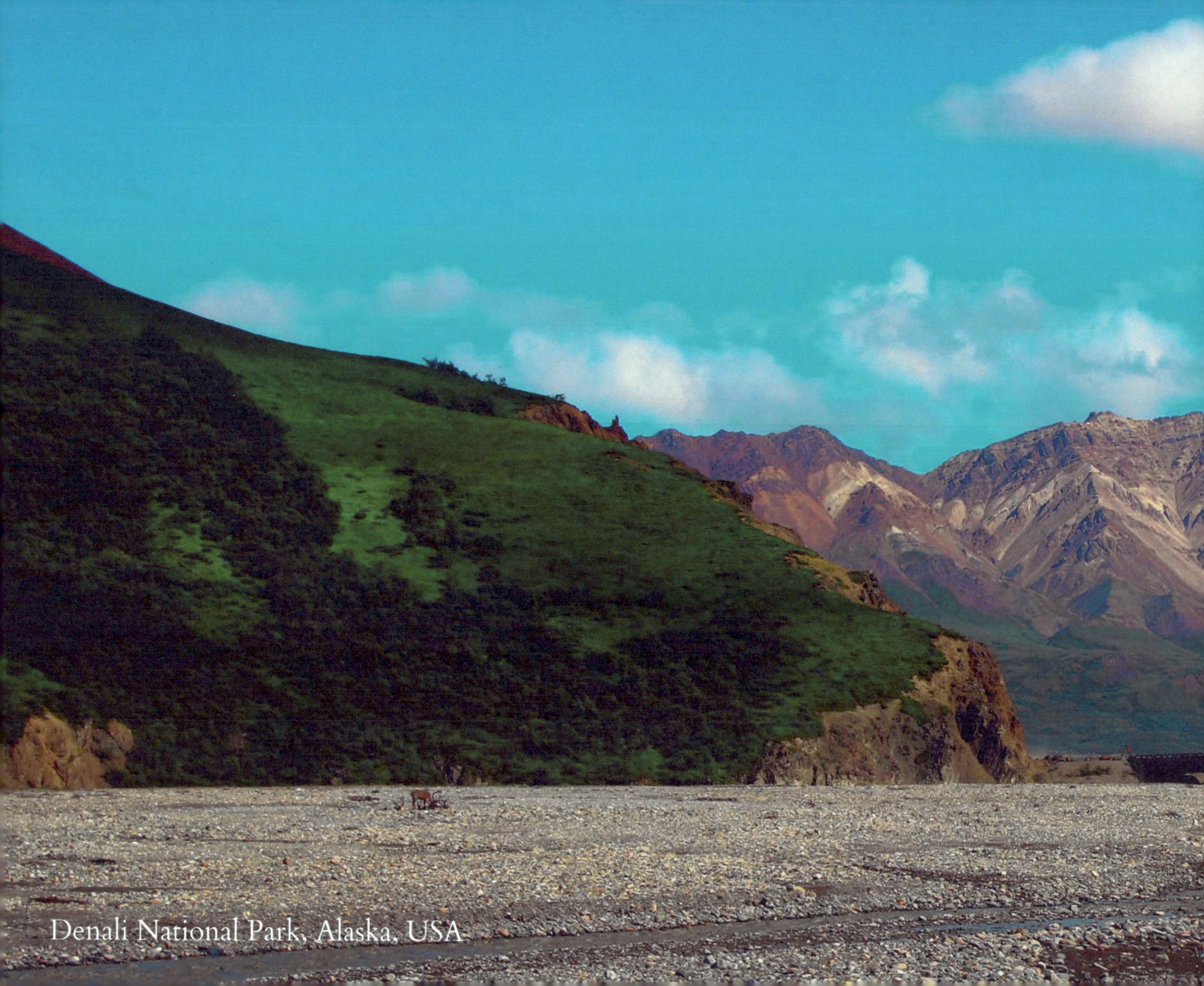

Denali National Park, Alaska, USA

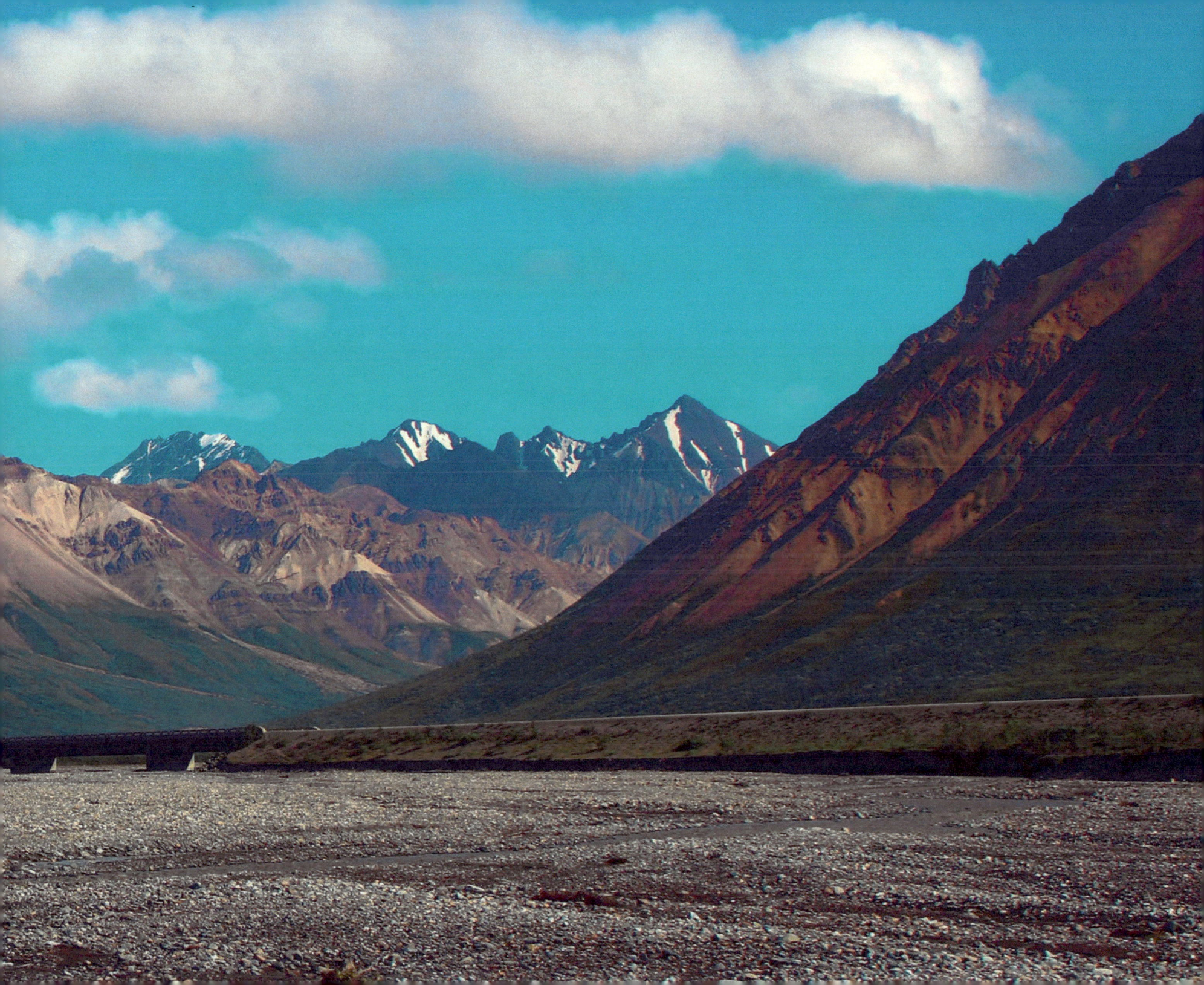

The human being is a perplexing thing. From the tips of our toes, to the very depths of our souls; we are unlike any other.

We don't co-exist, oh no, not even with each other.

We walk the earth as if we own it.

To each their own, we claim. Yet, we can't help but insert ourselves and our ways everywhere.

North, West, East and South; mankind has, without a doubt, spread its destruction, and laid its waste.

Without a thought, without remorse.

You see, we can't help it. We are greedy creatures.

We were made this way. Not by our Creator, but by this world, that we have bred on blood.

We were all born with hearts of gold, but die with souls so cold.

Irreparable, we are. Ungrateful. Unworthy.

But are we really? Shall we succumb to this horrifying reality? Or will we break free and make our stand?

Be it futile. Will we stand for all we see? Speak out as the free?

Or will you let your silence define you? Forever enslaved by the ideology of "what if?".

Silence is violence. Silence is compliance.

Make your stand.

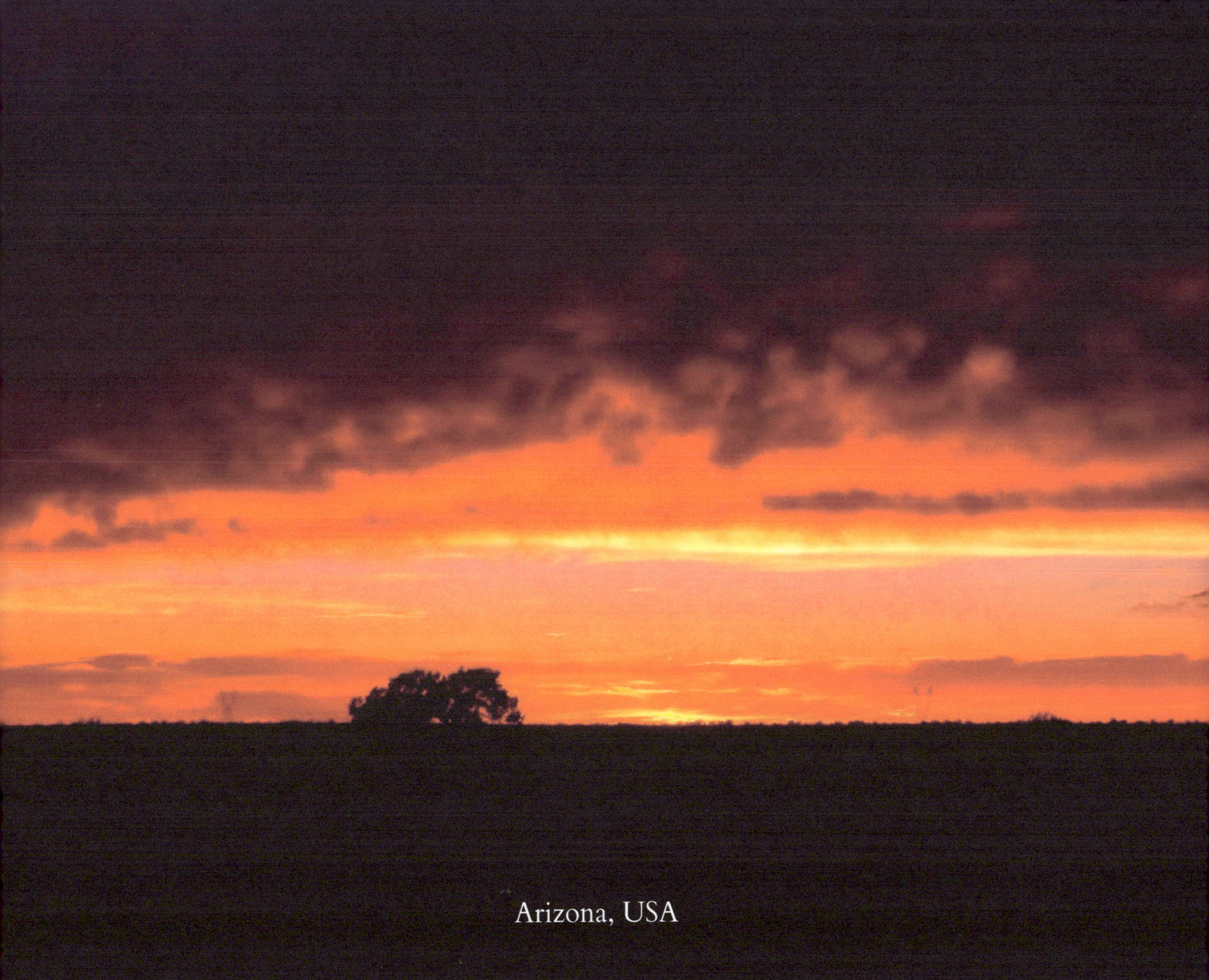

Arizona, USA

Every day, no matter how busy your schedule is, take some time out to do something you love; something you've always wanted to do. That thing at the very back of your mind that you're always delaying for the sake of deadlines and assignments.

Do the thing that everybody's probably telling you NOT to do only because it'll take away from whatever your commitments are. It'll make the rest of your tedious tasks more bearable and give you something to look forward to each day. Because, let's face it. While our responsibilities are important, you can't become a zombie fixated on your professional goals. It doesn't work that way at all, don't sell yourself to the system. Do your best, yes. Always do your best. But do what makes you happy, too.

Money and grades are important but are you just going to be another number on a spreadsheet or do you want to be a person with talents and achievements, personality and aspirations? Will you differentiate yourself, stand out and make your mark? Or just become another cog in the machine, making money for a superior who doesn't even know your name? Work on yourself, do what makes you happy.

Grow into a person, not a number.

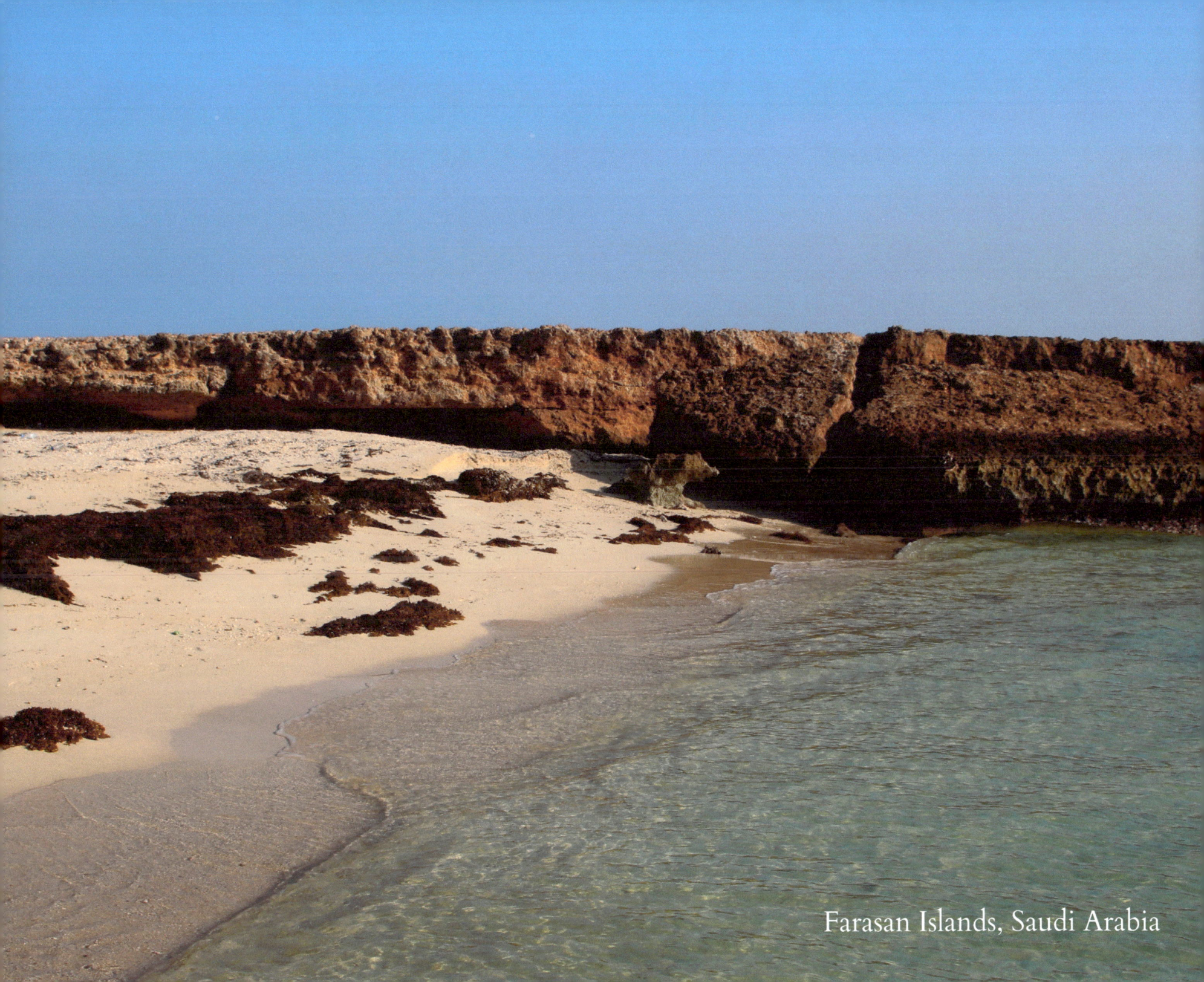

Farasan Islands, Saudi Arabia

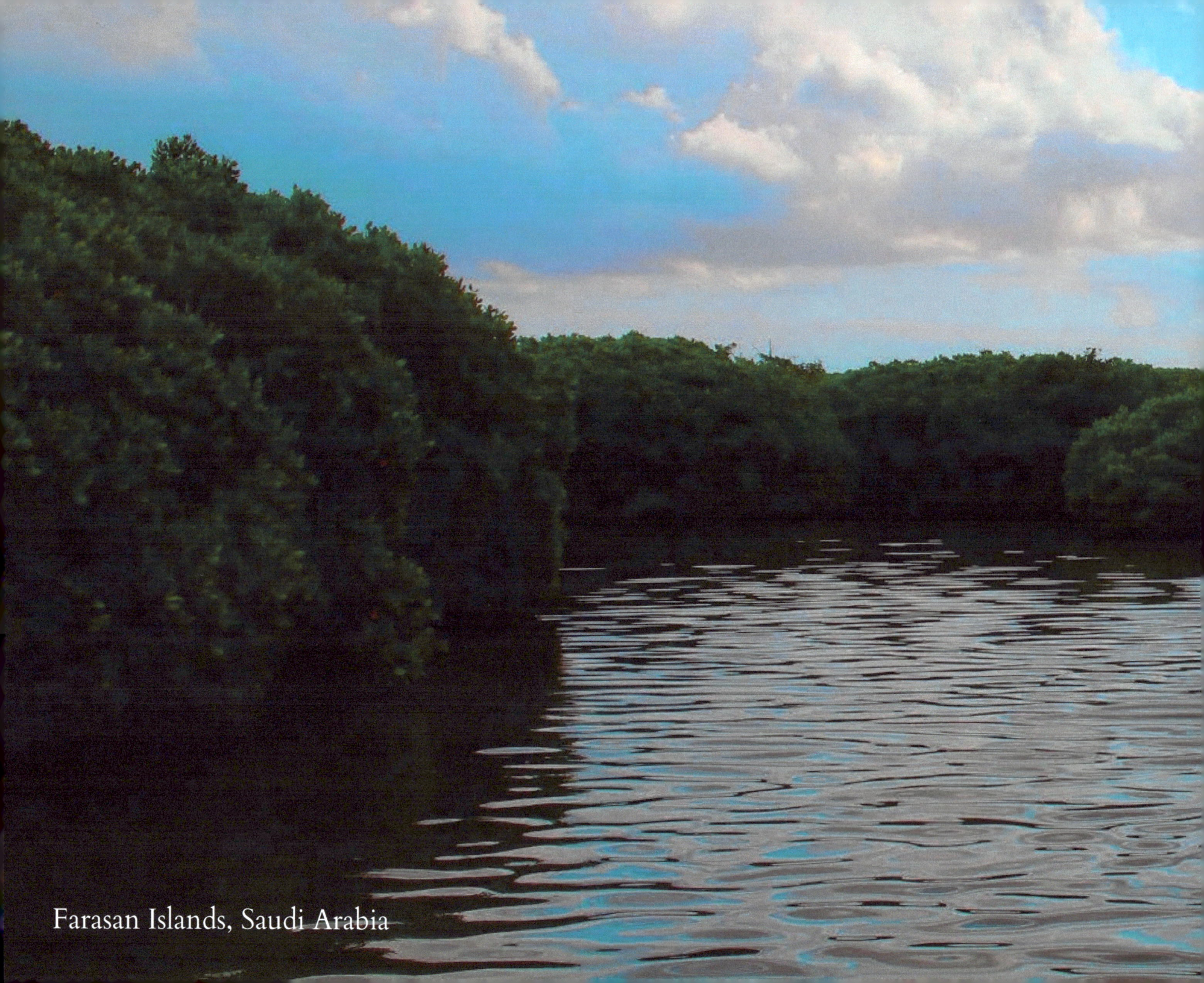

Farasan Islands, Saudi Arabia

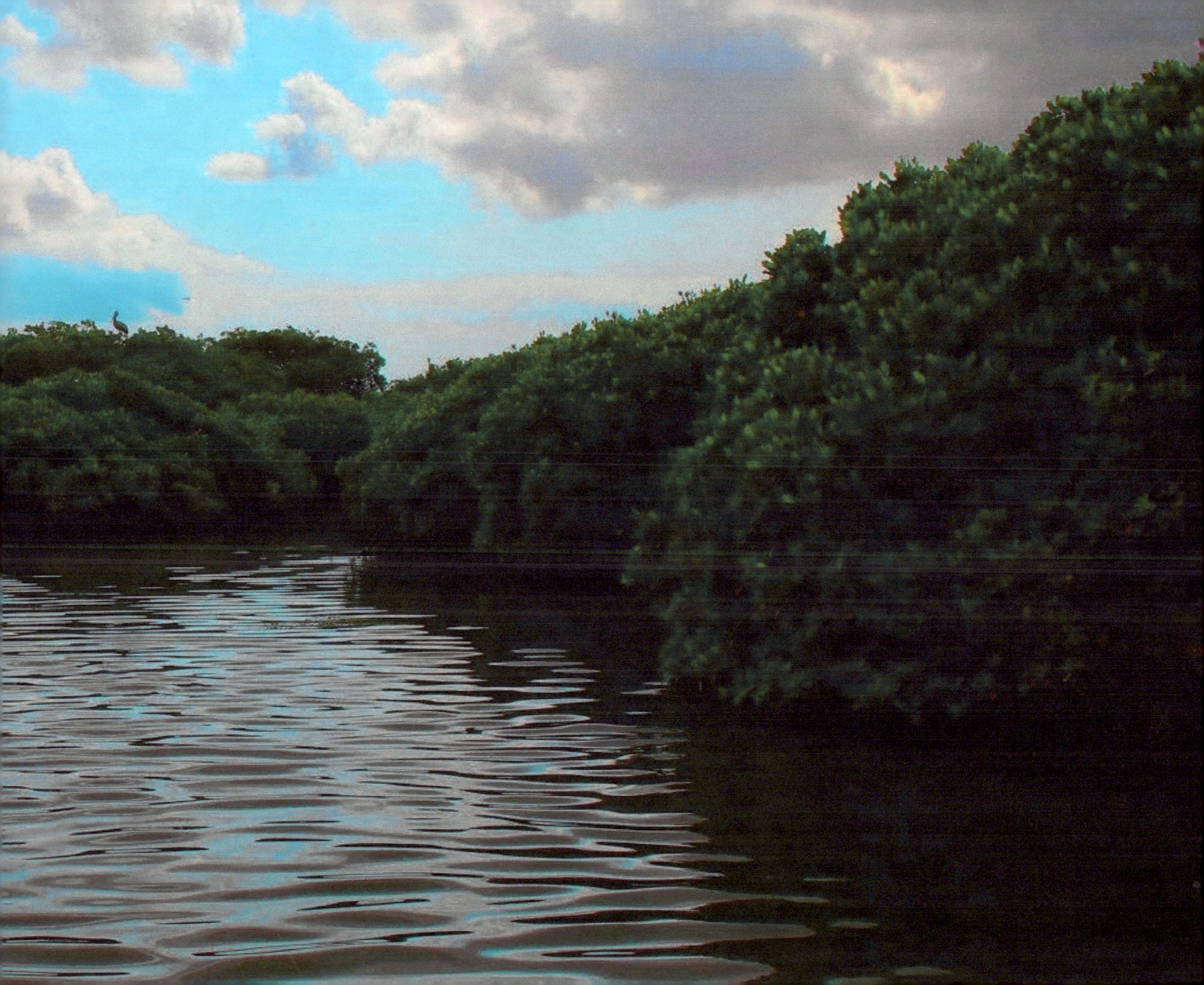

Cloudy days, always so mystical and magical.
When will we meet again? This waiting is maniacal.
Longing for the serenity I see in the clouds, I'm stuck with my thoughts;
forever unbound.
Sitting at my desk, I await the calm you bestow on our hearts.
Thinking of the pitter patter of water on the sidewalks.

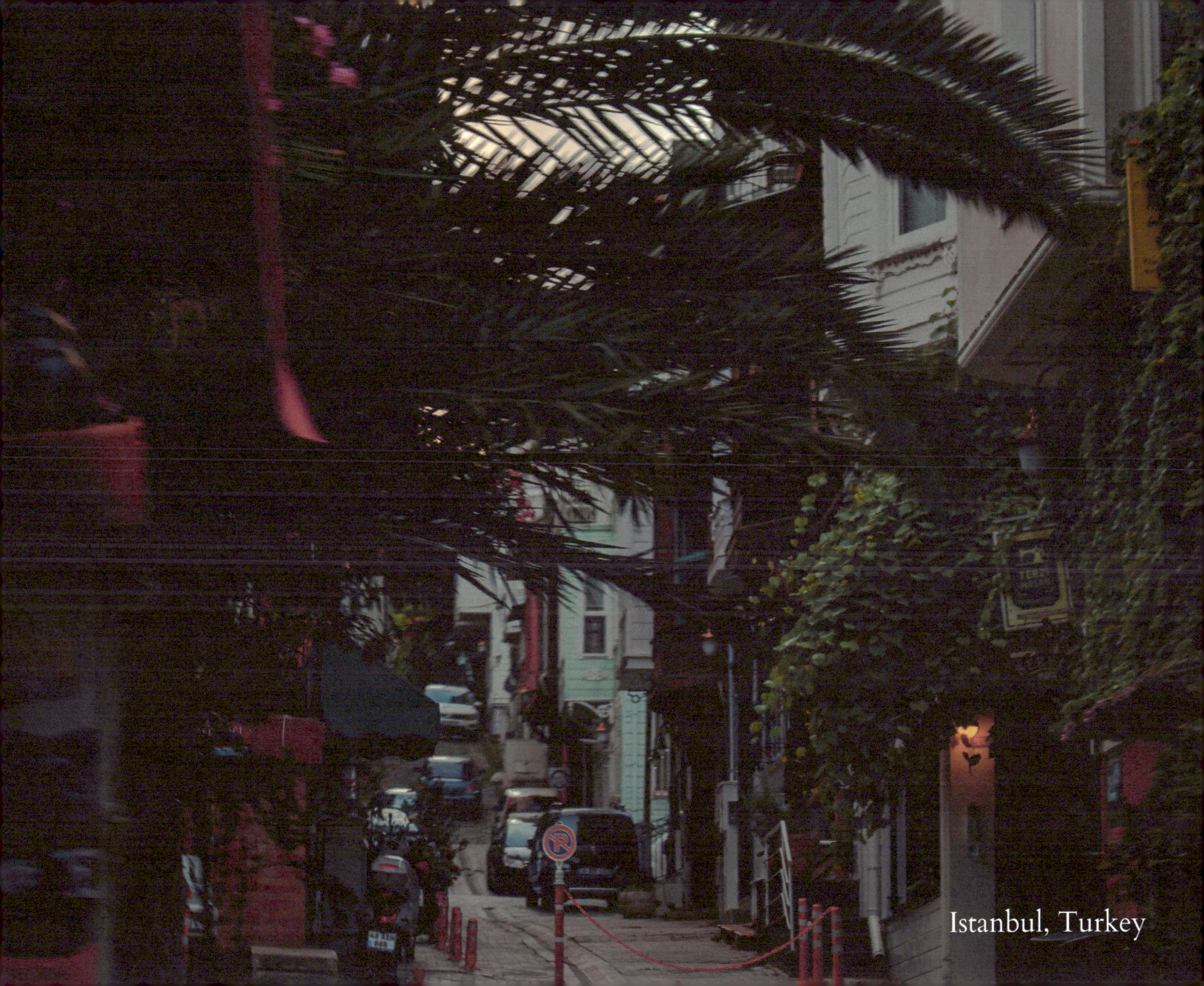

Istanbul, Turkey

Falling off the deep end
Head first into the never-ending sea
Farther and farther I go
Down, into my fears

Broken mirrors staring back at me
Horrendous smiles, peering down on me
My own face amongst the crowd, terrorizing me
The very thing I swore to never become
Is what fate had shaped my legacy to be

Looking around, they are all I can see
Closing in on me, until I can no longer breathe
Until I am no longer me.

Kanab, Utah, USA

I learnt a lot from my time in Pakistan.

I learnt that dedication and goodness in people can overcome anything. I learnt that it's the simple things that matter most, that nothing at all matters if you don't allow it to influence you. That you can be happy even if you're not surrounded by all the riches of the world. That what you wear, where you come from or what tongue you speak doesn't matter at the end of the day because we're all one in the same. I learnt that there's a kindness in some people that is rare and gifted and to hold onto it is even harder. But I also realized some of the common themes that plague all underdeveloped countries. We know the people are underserved, with private companies and charities having to carry the burden instead of the government the people put their trust in. We know there is crime, atrocities, disease and illiteracy.

There is still immense work that needs to be done. People aren't educated or aware, the common man walks into the ER having no idea whether he's suffering from a fatal illness or a common cold. Our countries – "back home" – have so much good, but also a fair amount of bad. And to overcome that bad, we need to change. Not just as a society or a nation, but on an individual level. So that when you do reach a position of power, you can think about the stranger next to you; help out, give back, be kind, and raise awareness If we don't do something now, countless people will have to pay a price that should never have been theirs. Countless already have.

Don't be afraid to be the change you want to see.

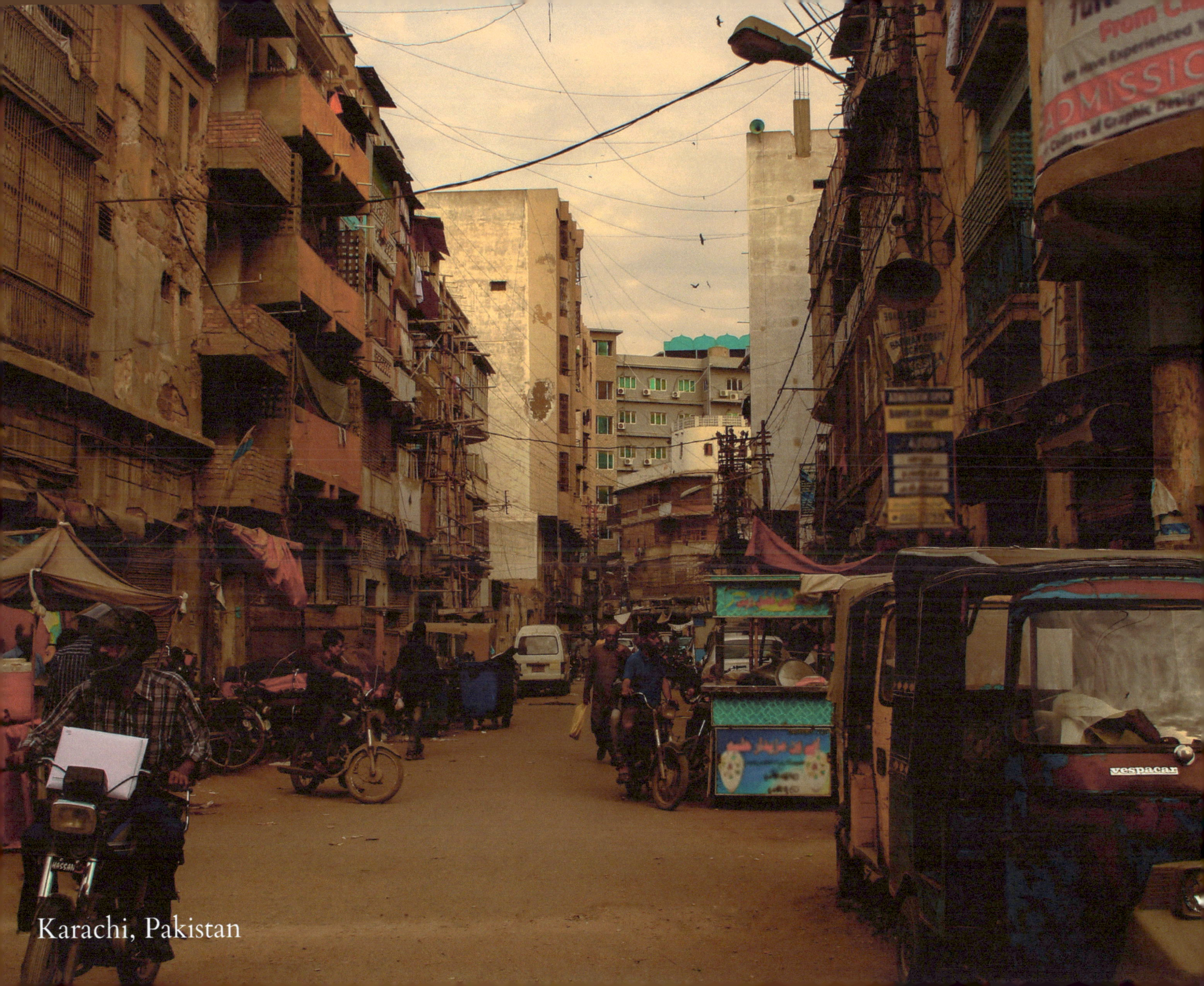
Karachi, Pakistan

Summer drives and traffic jams
Salty air and the sea's breeze
Music blasting through the radio
Notes floating out to sea
Unique among the masses and their beats
Don't you miss the wonders of summertime's feels?

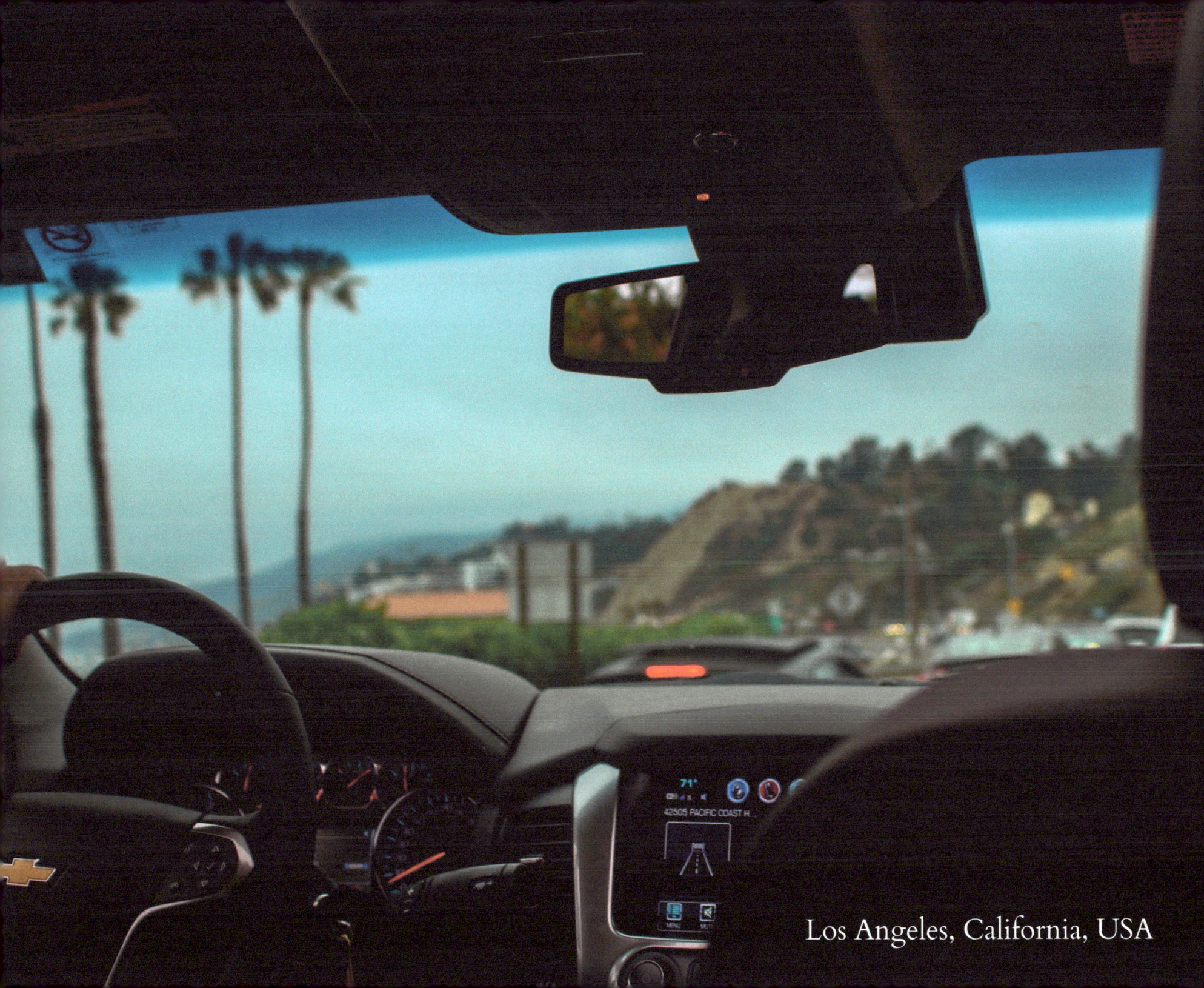

Los Angeles, California, USA

Do you ever just stare at the sky and reminisce? Imagine all that we have missed?

Or is it just me, that spends her days stuck deep, in a vicious cycle of what could have been?

Do you ever wonder what could have been done, had you shouted at the top of your lungs, instead of running to a place forgotten by the tons?

Is it truly just me, in doubt of every deed I have done in the past few years?

Hours spent in front of the sun, burnt until I am no longer stunned, yet not a second goes by in this world forged by a smoking gun.

Standing there, alone and weak, I plead as the bright yellow orb sinks to a place so deep, even those who have been rendered bleak cannot see.

A mixture of red and blue, a million different hues, break over the sky now born anew.

The moon and the stars, shining from afar, hoping we do not fall.

Granting the lost a home for their thoughts.

Transfixed as I am, I move unconsciously back to my spot, and spend the rest of my night, staring at the stars.

Awaiting the return of the blasted star that oversaw us until we got to where we are.

But, until then, I wonder in awe;

"Is it just me, who looks up at the stars, and ponders over who we truly are?"

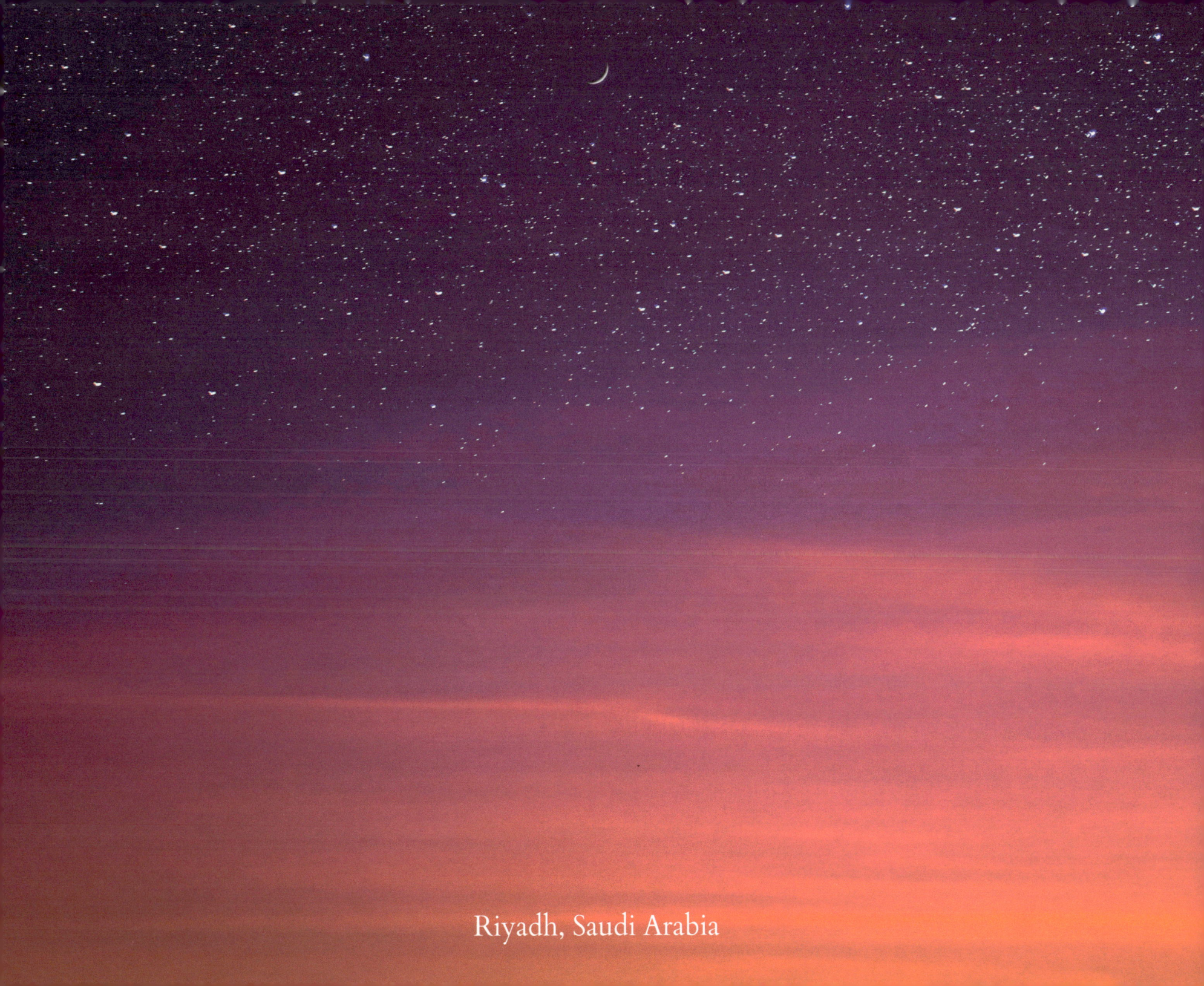

Riyadh, Saudi Arabia

A Flickering Vision

Candle light flickering in my reflection
Wax dripping onto my hands, pain going unregistered
Mighty mountains yawning beyond our tiny existence
A silent witness to all the horrors that have been afflicted

Do you ever just wonder
What you have done to deserve such plunder?
The world that has turned its back on us
Is to blame for all the floating dust
Yet not a single one of them remembers us
Only on this solemn occasion they call "black day"
Do they do so to calm their own consciences into a lull
To do right, a mere publicity stunt

I do not believe I can ever find inner peace
Not with the police on every street
Watching us as wolves do sheep
Prowling this sacred land as if it was theirs to keep

But, if that is the price I must pay
Then no amount of pain is too steep
To see my people finally free

Candle diminishing, fears culminating, anger overspilling
I take in my reflection, a portrait of survival
My mere existence, a witness statement
As is all of ours, enigmas to the system

Defiance in our every breath
Resistance to the threat
And only on the day we are free from the distress
Will we take a moment to pause, and reassess
But until then, we are survivors that do not rest
Not until our land is ours, by God's Will, once again

—From the perspective of an anonymous Kashmiri girl—

The stains on their kameez match those left on our land prior to our peace,
The grace with which they carry their feet, matches the way our nation
swept into a hurry to succeed,
All that work just to make ends meet, while the rest of the country has the
world before their feet,
Yet, none raise their hand to provide ease.
Is it that we think we are better than those who carry our fleets?
Treating them as if they are beneath our feet,
Too busy trying to appease those across the sea, too busy to notice we are
diseased,
To remember we are all one breed,
And that we have become exactly what they hoped us to be,
From the day they realized we have nothing left to milk,
Everything we had, gone on their ships.
To build their own up until we were the ones left with nothing but sticks,
Piling up their bricks so high none can peek,
Walls made of the money and sweat they took from us while we stare in awe
like sheep.
Have we just become what they intended us to be?
Or have we brought this fate upon ourselves by our own greed?

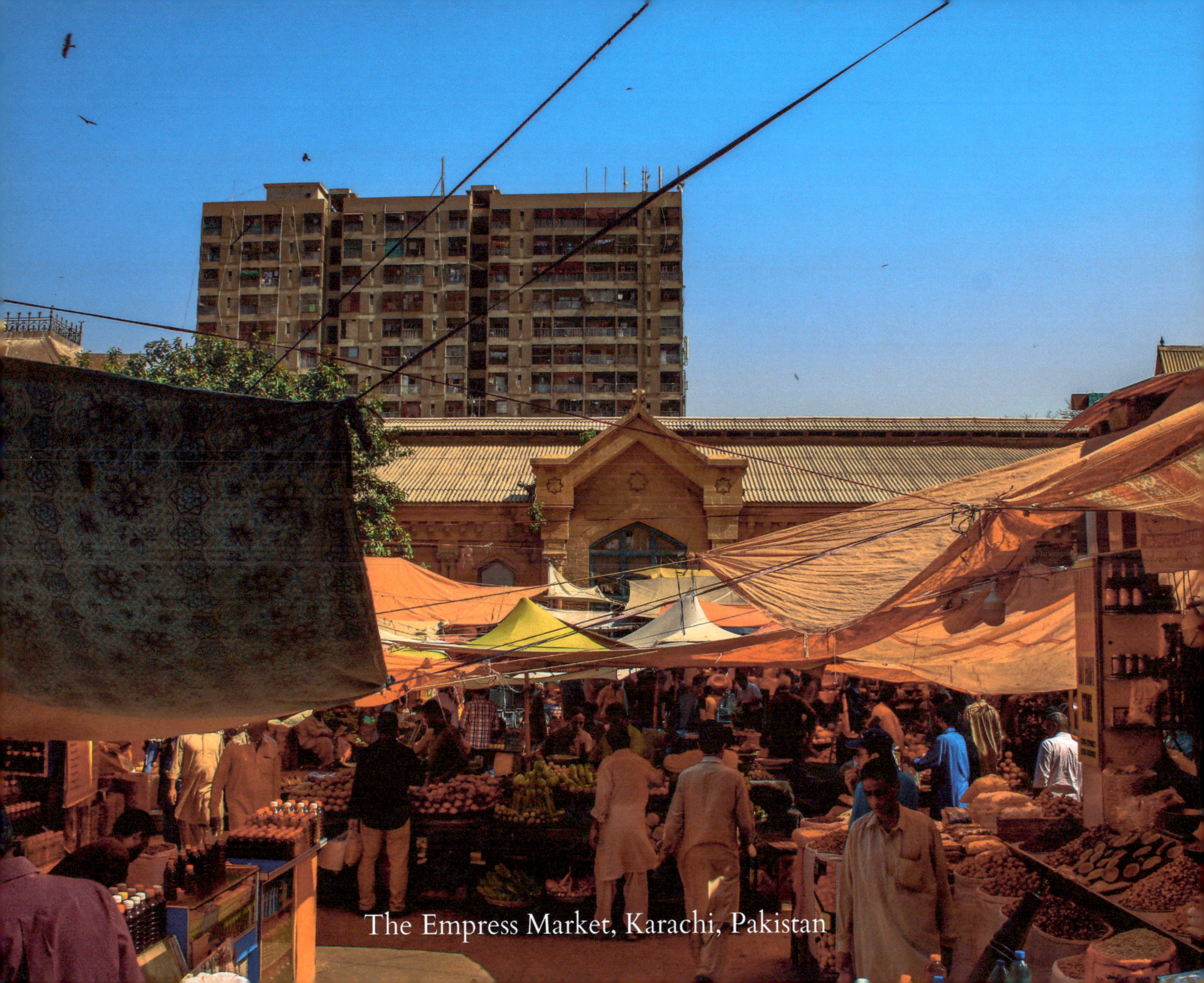

The Empress Market, Karachi, Pakistan

When the winds change,
And bring with them times of grief
Do you still remember me?

All the days we spent together in the sun
The times we had; oh such fun
Do you still remember them?

I bear with me, everyday
A shadow on my heart
Of the times I've prayed
For days like these
When I've finally grown up

But, now I realize
It was all a dream
And I've finally woken up
To the world in it's truth
With all its horrors and trials

How I long for the days
Spent with not a worry in sight

I spend my remaining days
Reminiscing of that depthless slumber
That I wish to fall into once more and for all

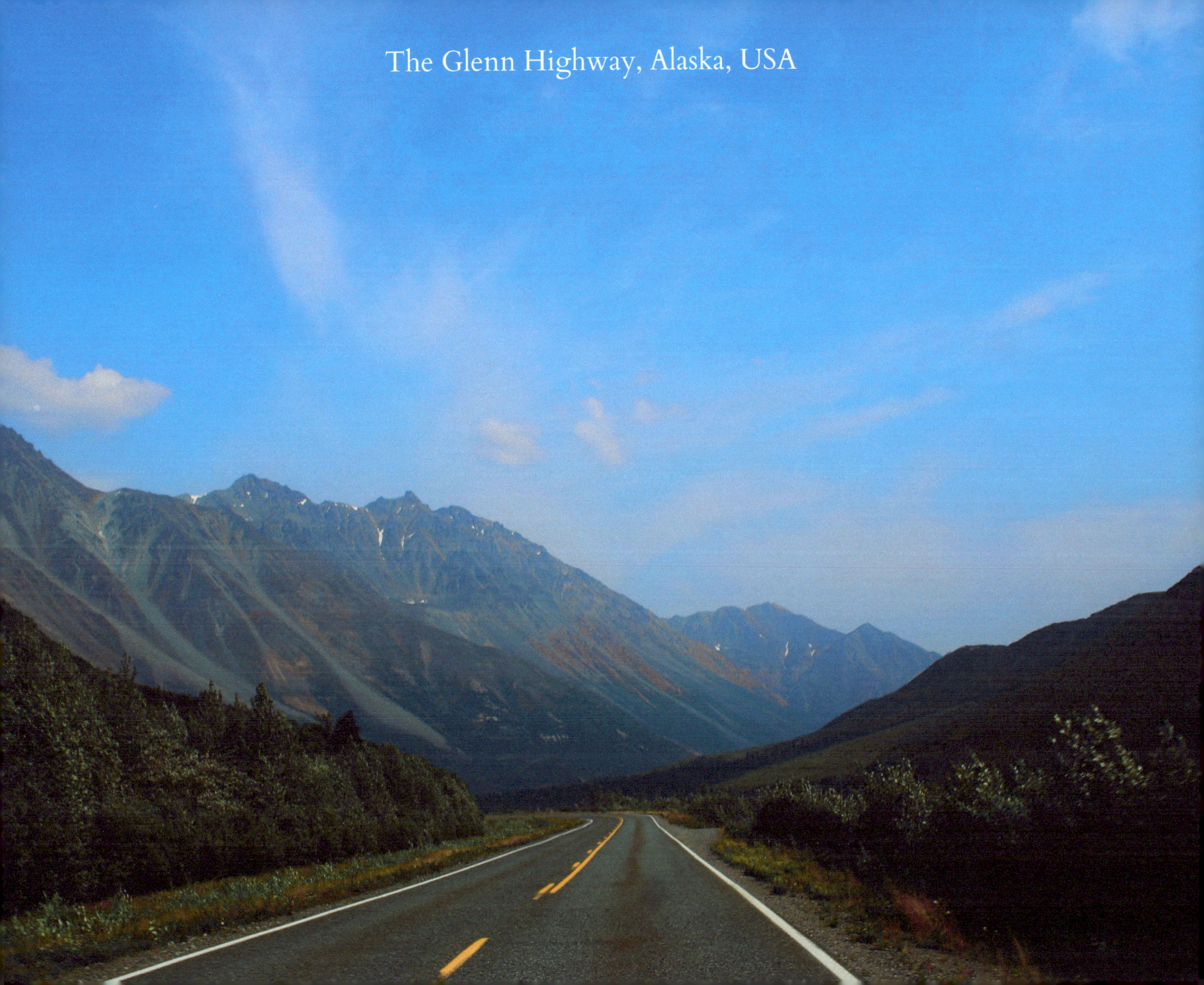

The Glenn Highway, Alaska, USA

What you may see is something beautiful; the rush of fresh, cold water into the sea. Great bergs of ice once built upon those mountains for millennia, seeing the world grow, evolve and change—finally joining the circle of life. But what I see is an imminent doom. A fate so terrible and so close it shocks me. Our doom is slowly and slowly creeping closer, yet the human race remains in collective oblivion. Not by force, oh no. Everything is laid right in front of us yet we are so selfish, so self-serving, that we refuse to do anything. Incessant bombing of the innocent, terrorization of children, the destruction of homes and sacred places.

We have taken far more than is our share, and in doing so, have abused and destroyed and laid waste to not just this planet but to ourselves. This terrible disease has swept the globe into silence, into hiding—but so much was going wrong before it because we didn't care enough to act. Now forced into the cages of our own homes, we are birds whose wings have been clipped. What will remain is up to us. It's now in our hands, to listen and take heed and get better. Else we go back to our toxic and vicious cycles and run this world into the ground, shying away from our sins until we are forced to account for them.

And what a reckoning that shall be.

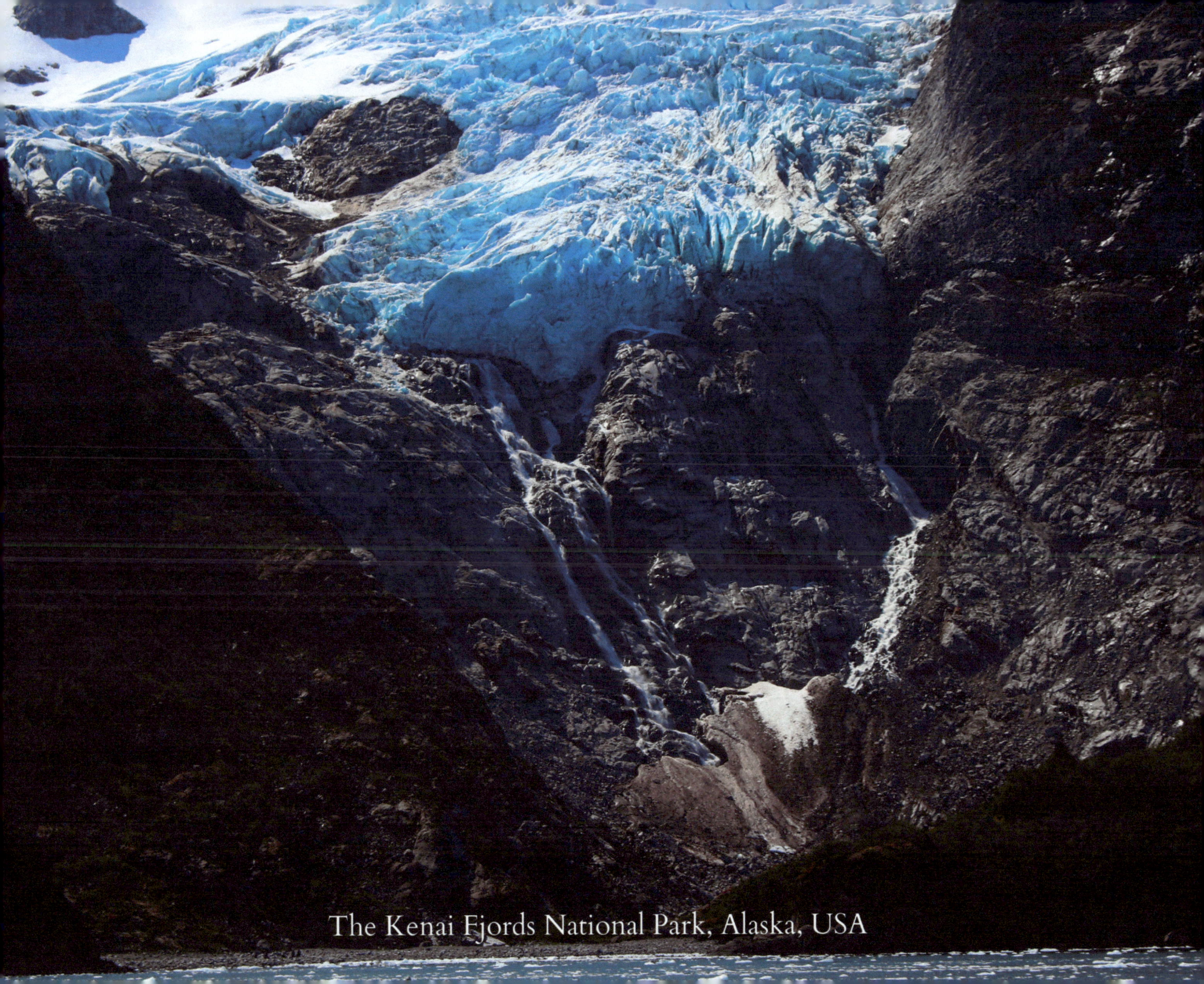
The Kenai Fjords National Park, Alaska, USA

The night has never changed.
It shifts through a gloom of black and blue, and when the day breaks,
a purple hue takes over the sky anew.

With the night often comes a watchful entity. A reserved presence
that has accompanied the souls of lone men for centuries.
Yet, out of all bodies alien to us, it is a reassurance to our restless
hearts, most constant to our faults, with a careful gaze as our souls take
flight. To the stars and beyond.

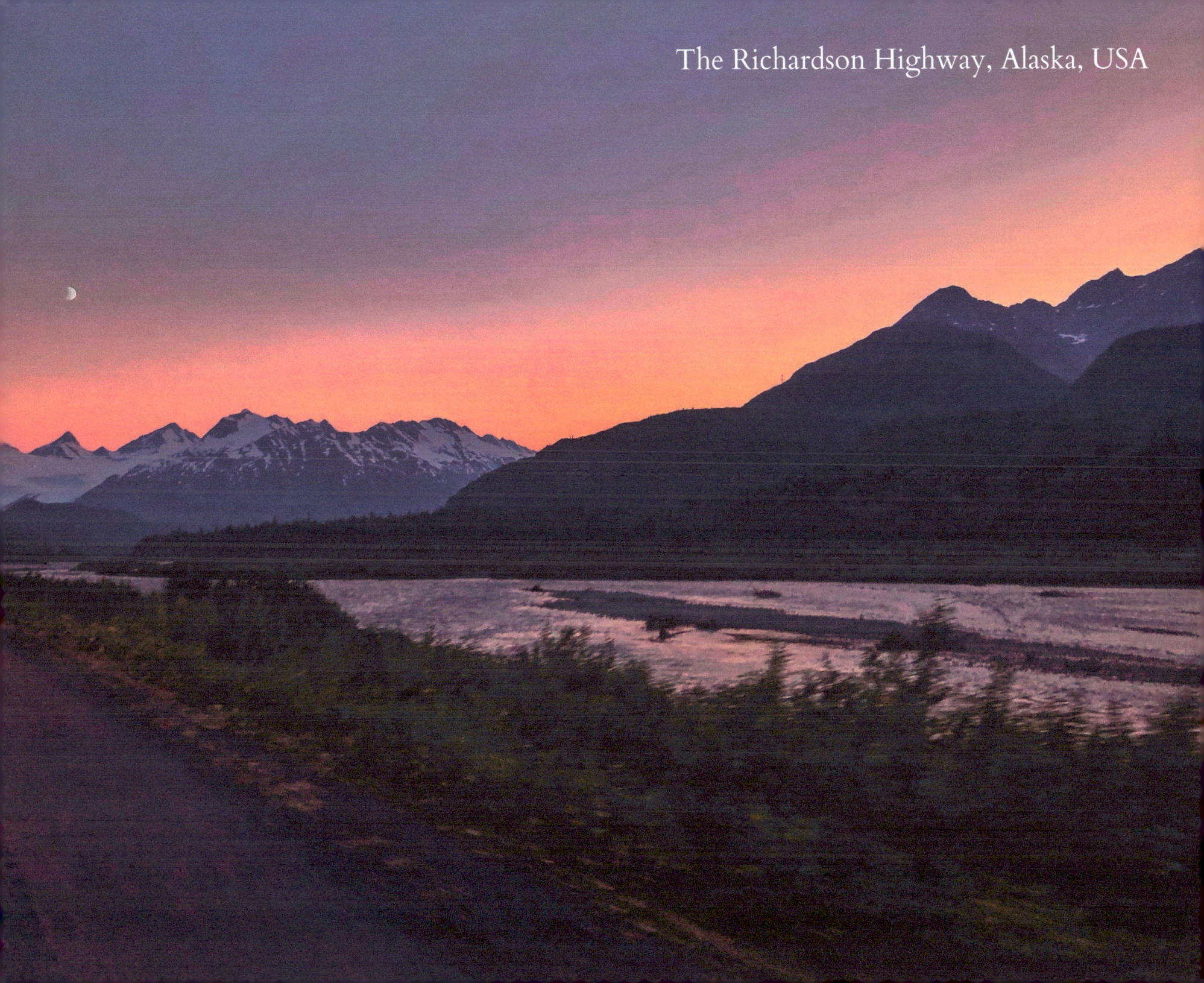

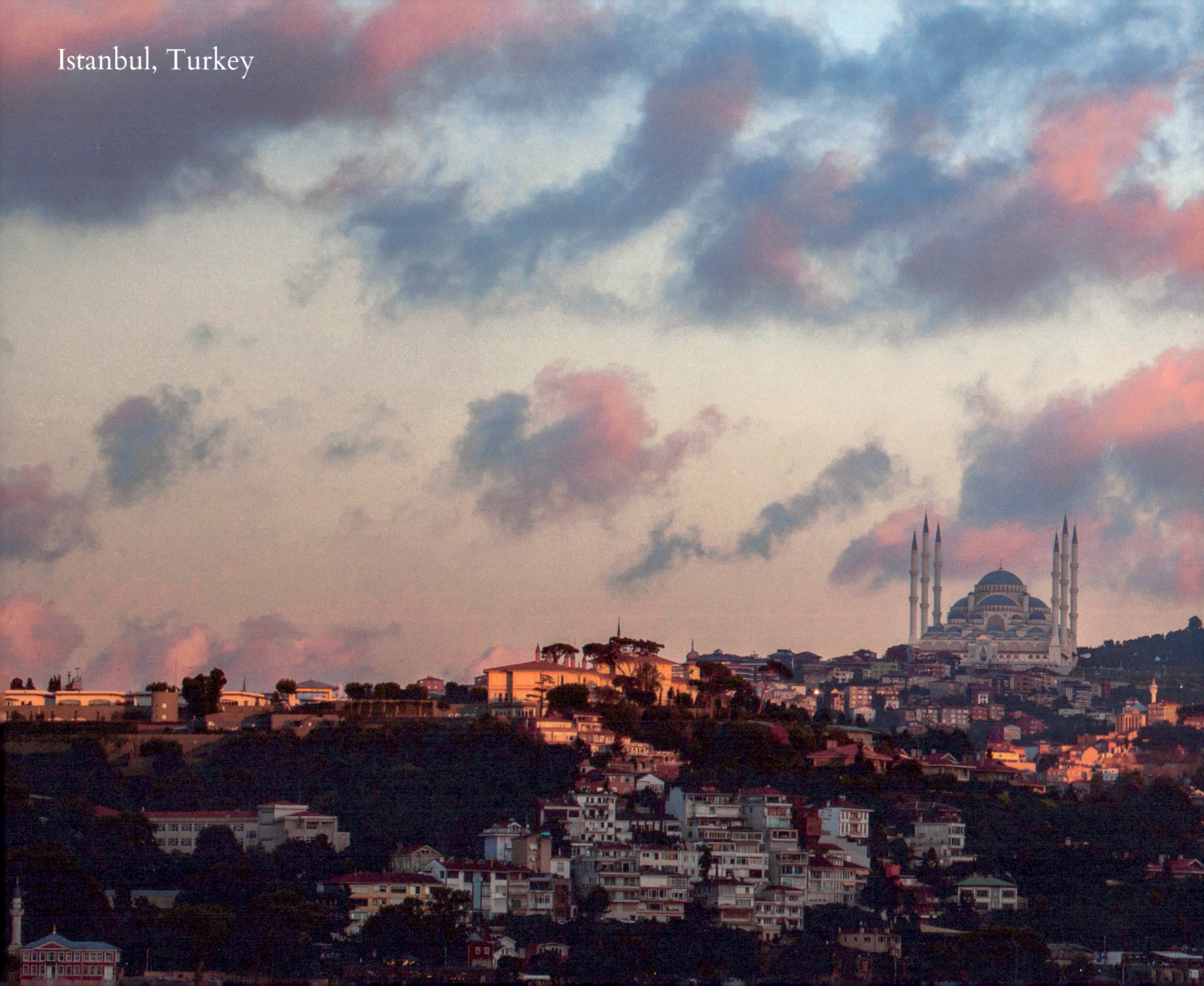

Istanbul, Turkey

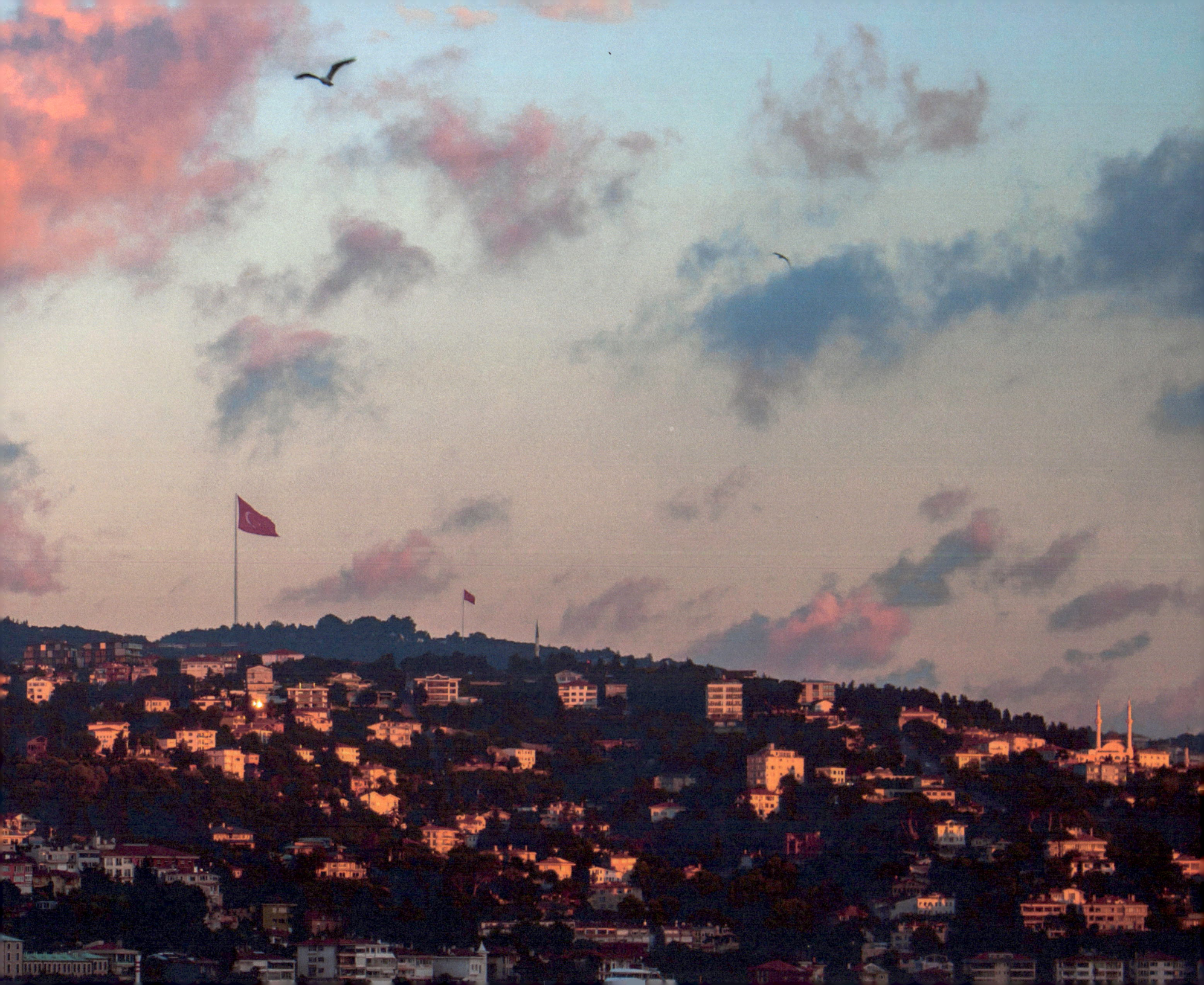

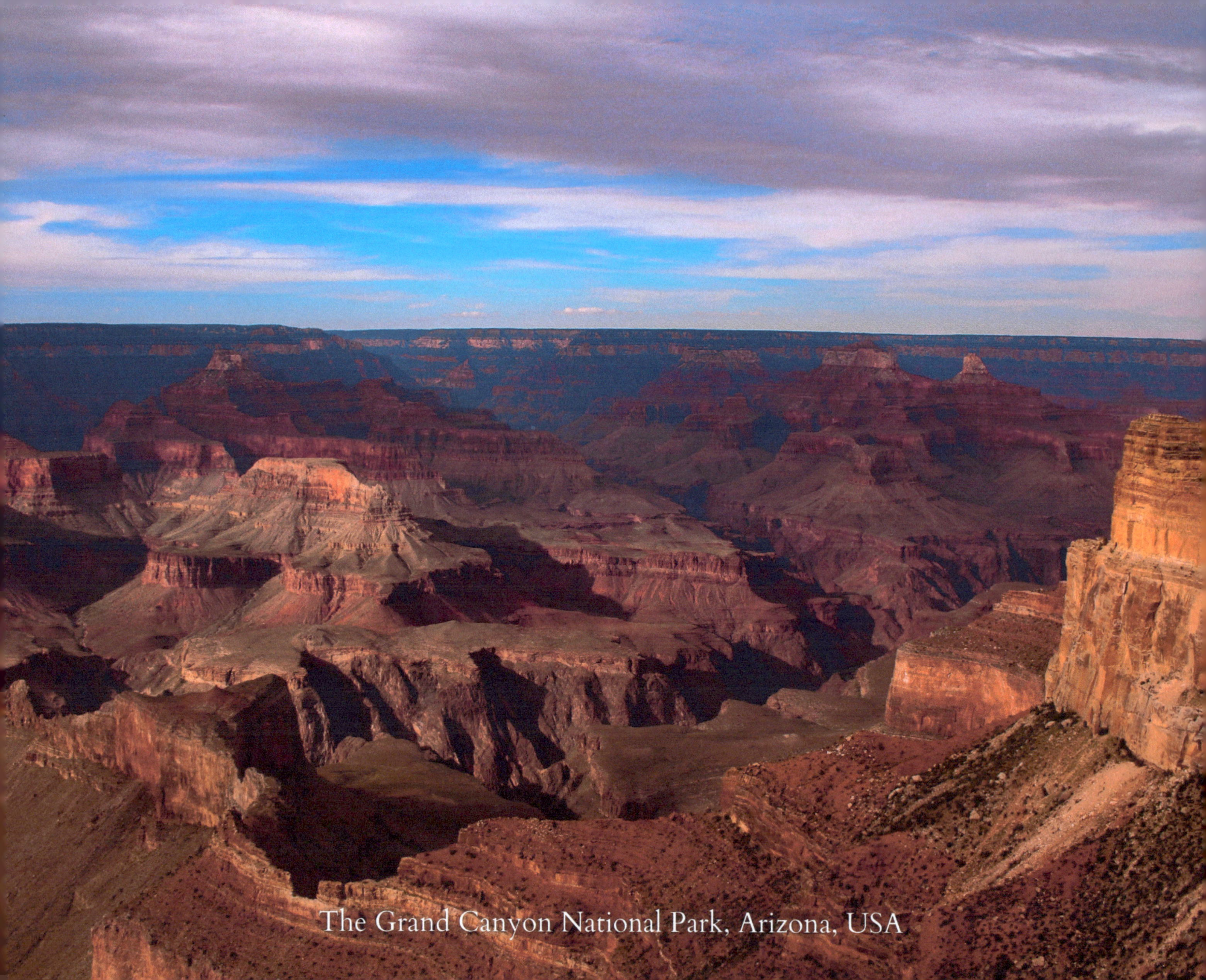

The Grand Canyon National Park, Arizona, USA

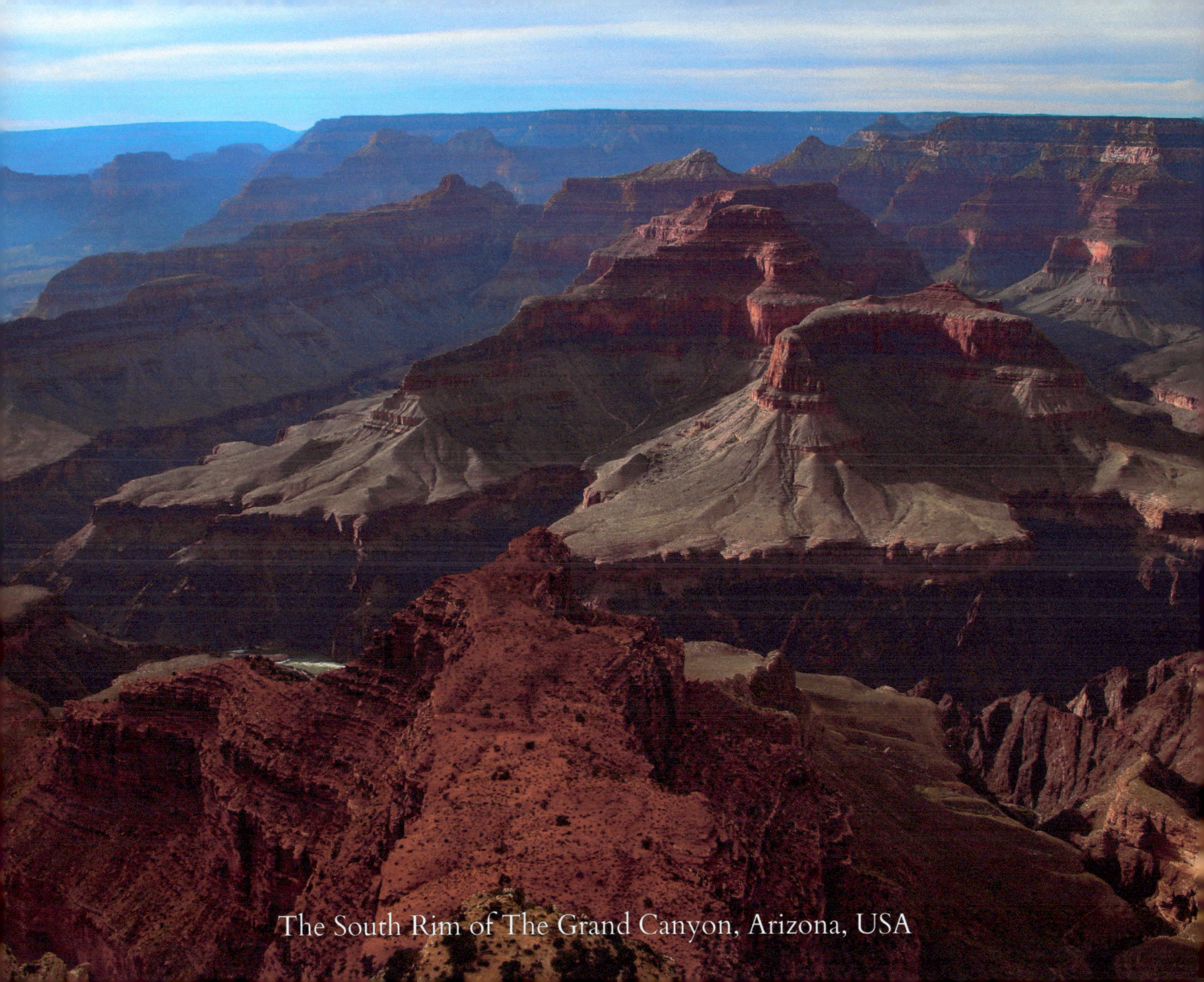

The South Rim of The Grand Canyon, Arizona, USA

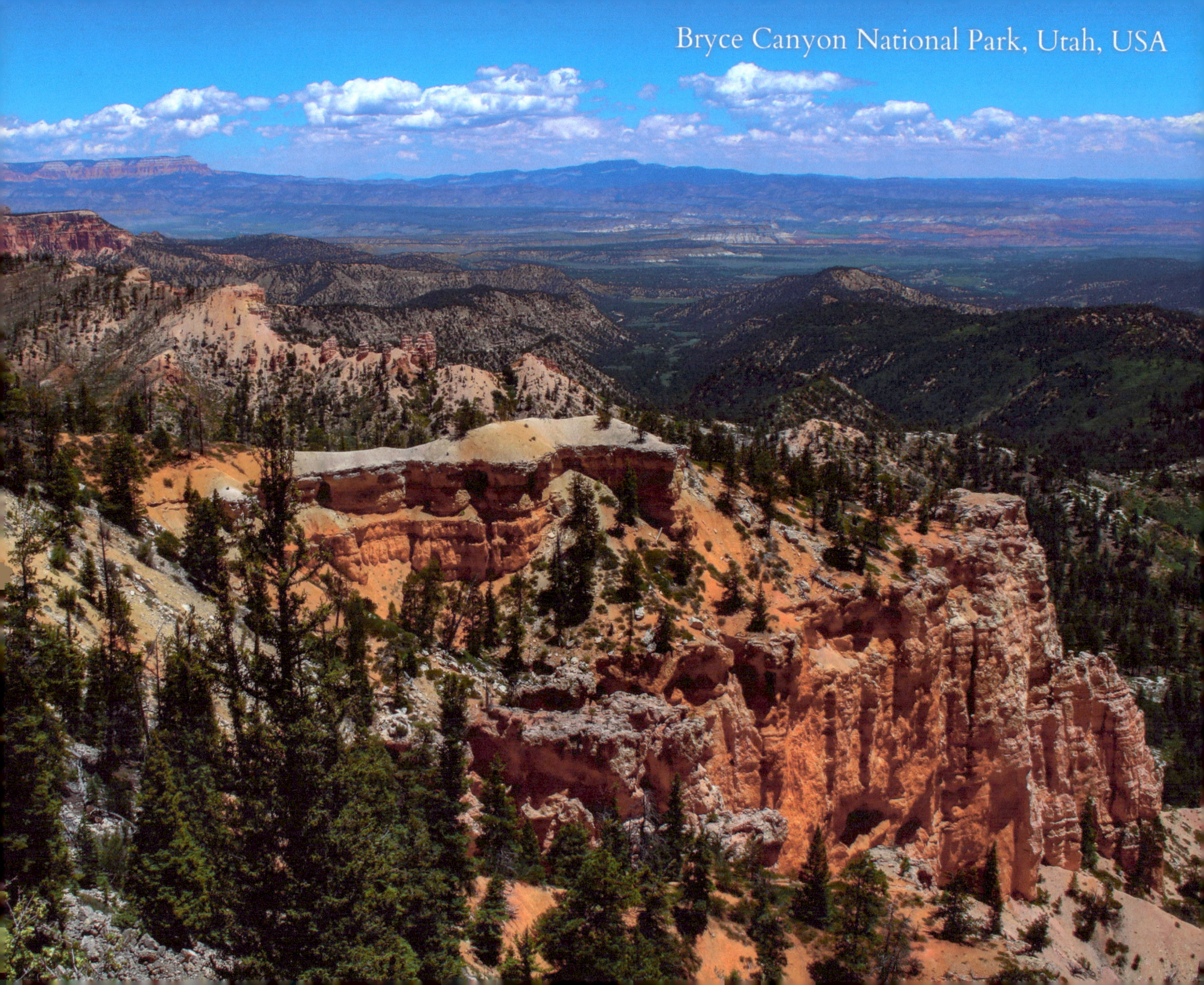
Bryce Canyon National Park, Utah, USA

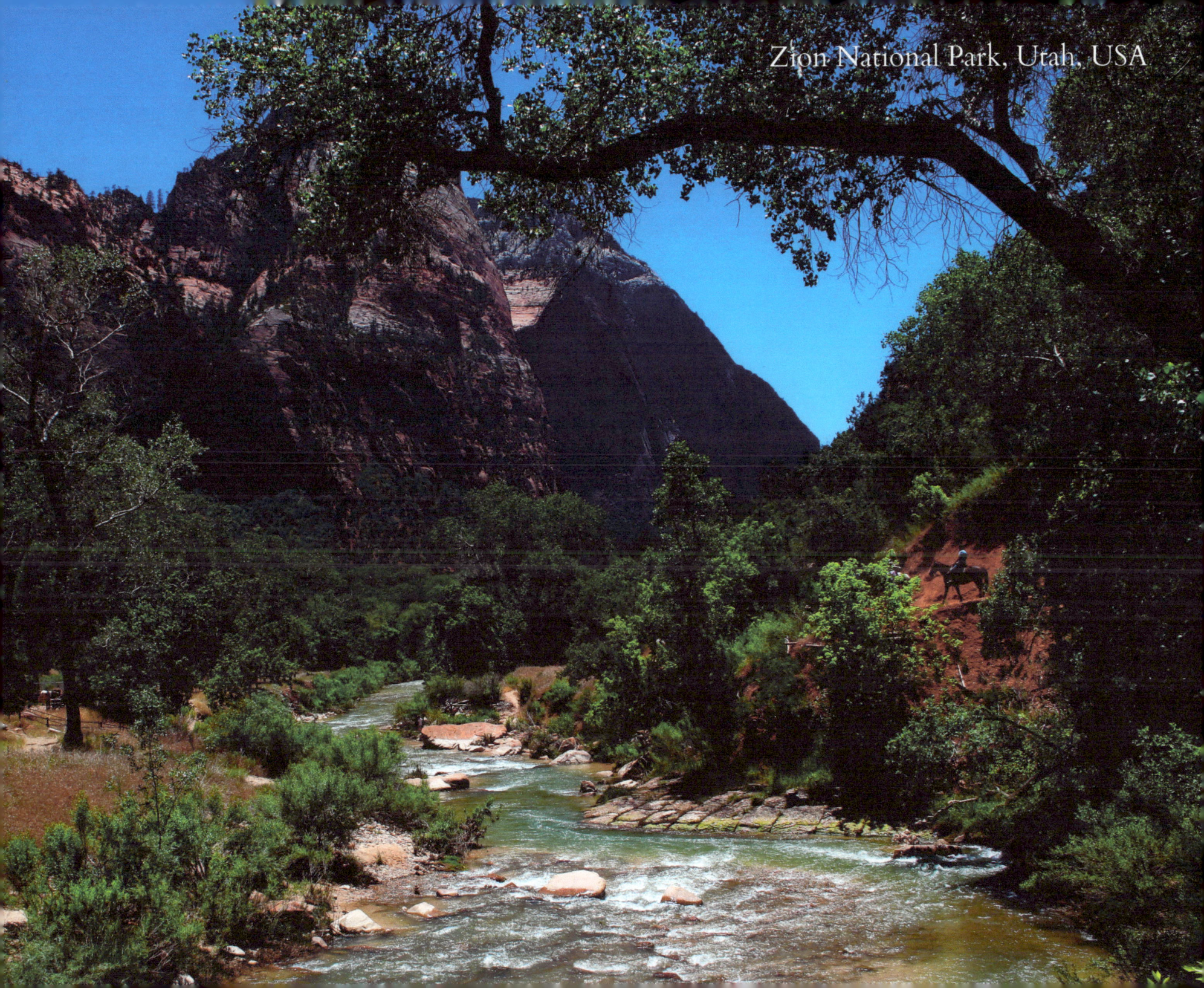

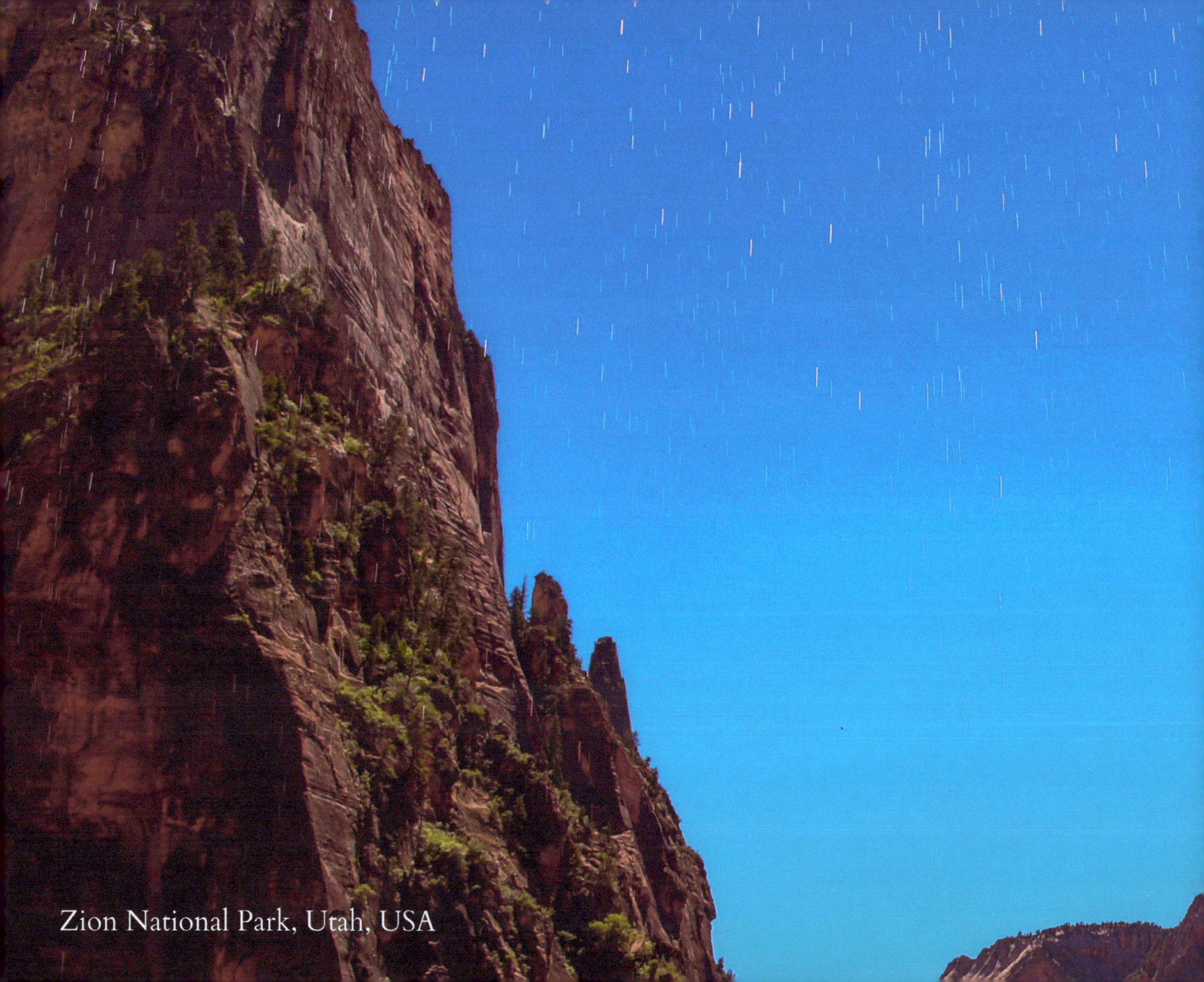

Zion National Park, Utah, USA

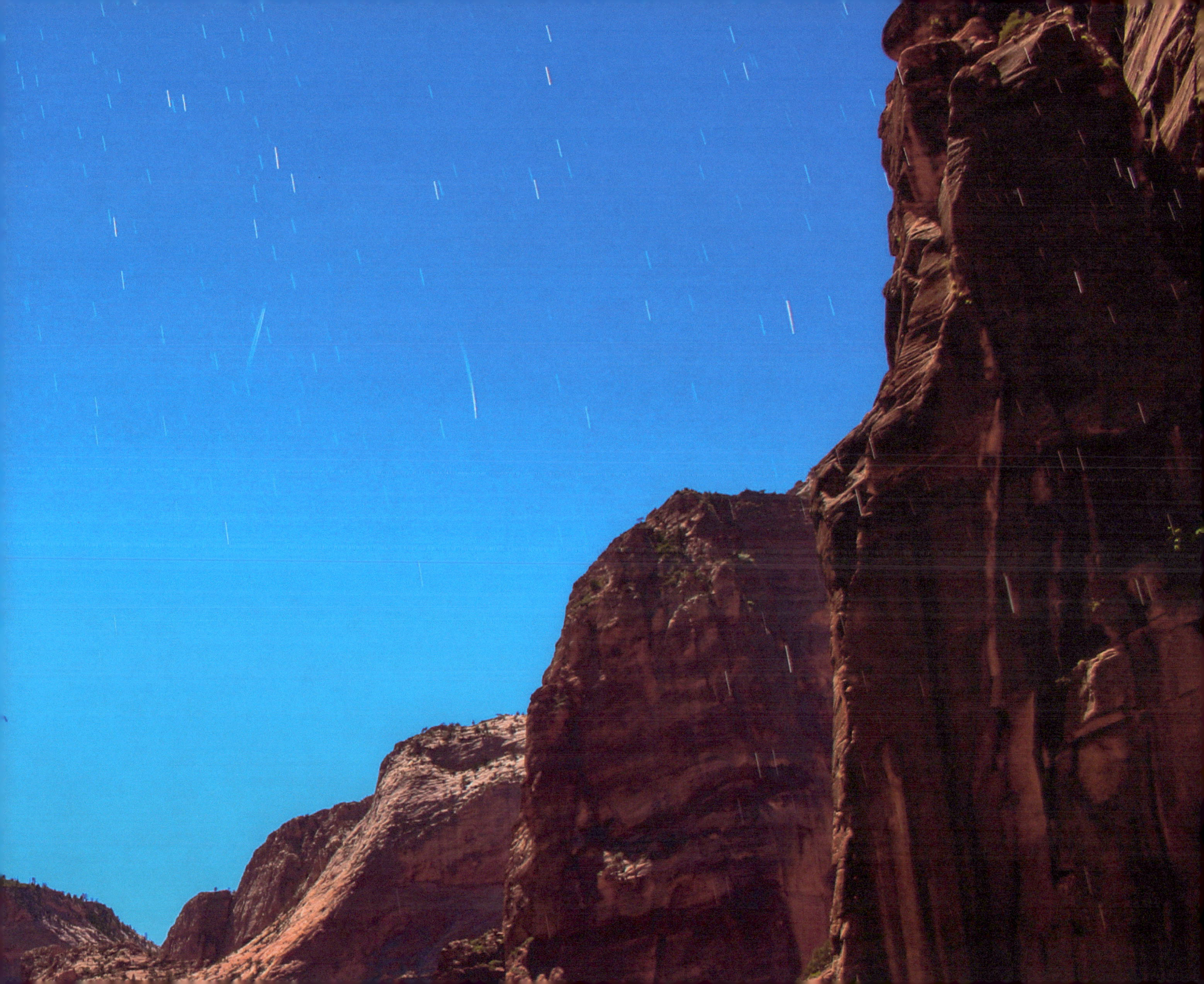

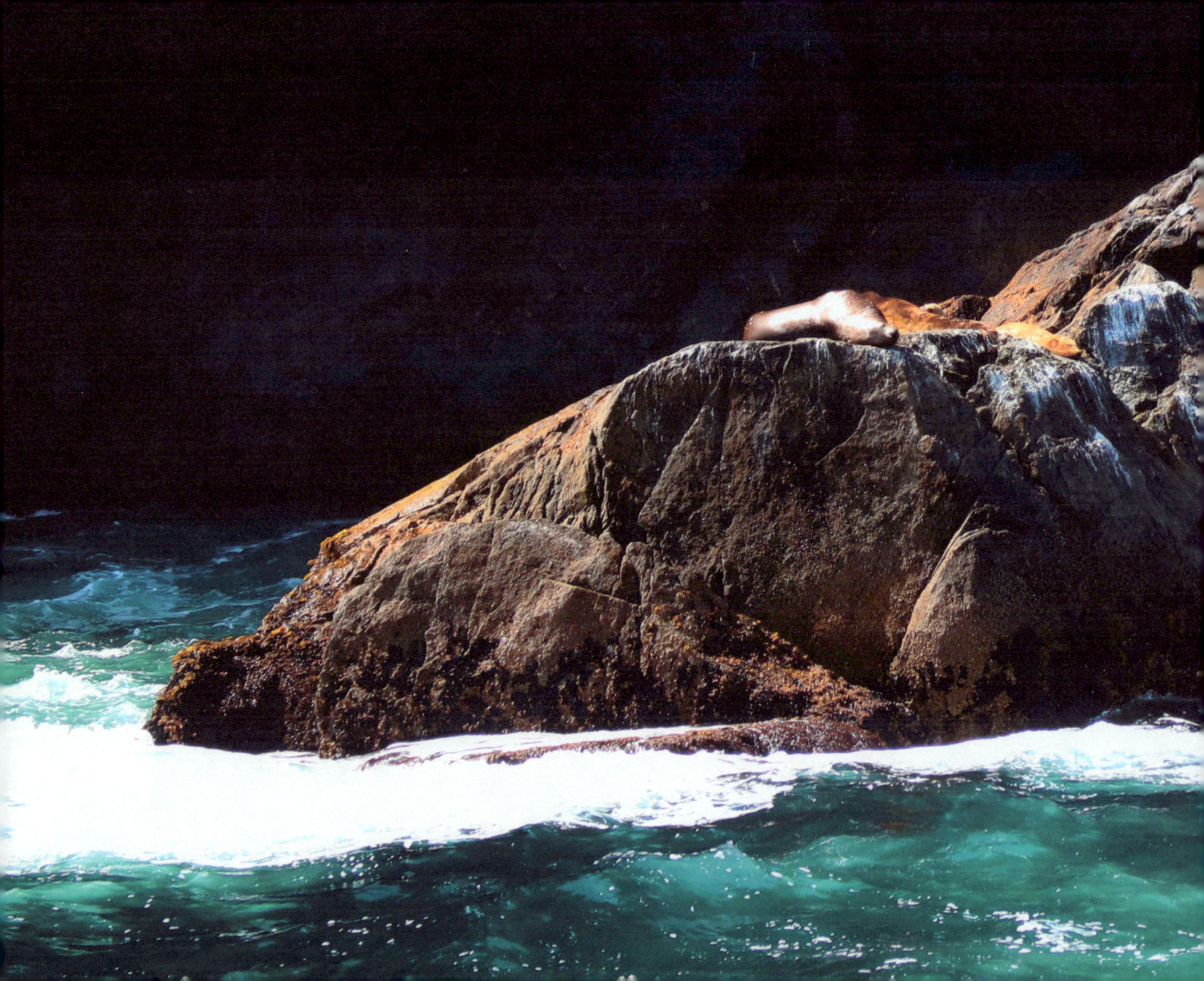

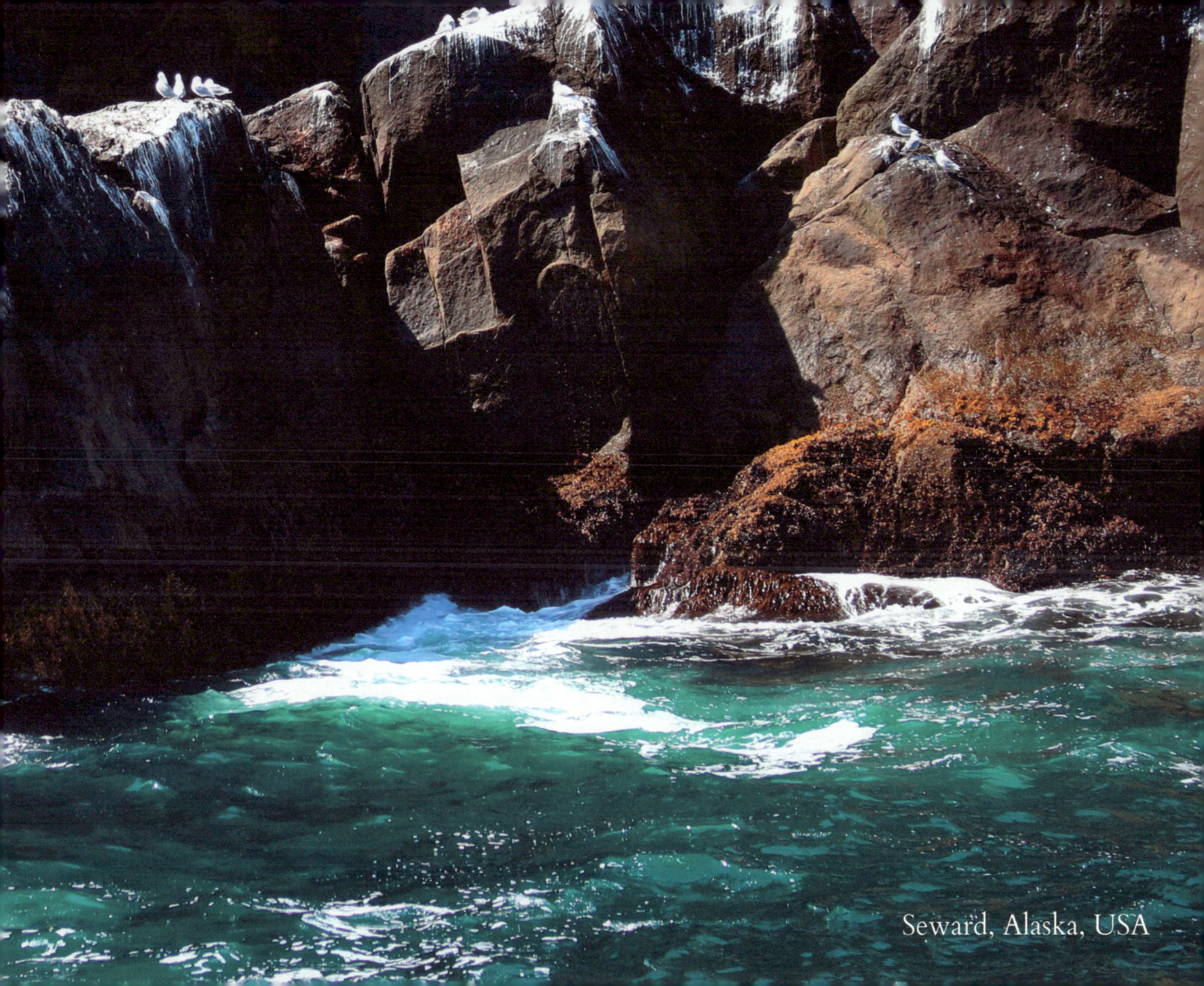

Seward, Alaska, USA

I never thought we'd be in this pandemic for this long. In the beginning, I was adamant on using my time productively. Yet, as this nightmare stretched farther than I imagined, I lost my motivation as did many others. I'm still beating myself up everyday for not meeting a study goal or waking up on time, but it's ok to not be at your best right now. It's ok to take a breather and do nothing. It's ok to not be ok. To those who feel as though our entire world has been turned upside down. We can't seem to focus on anything "productive" like we're being told to. "Utilize this time well," "get a head start." If you are managing all this, amazing for you but a lot of us are not. I don't think I have ever been this raw before, none of this is okay and it's hard. I'm tired of this stretching on and I'm tired of people pretending like it's over. It's not. People are dying. We have a responsibility to do our part not just for ourselves, but everyone else too. Since so many have lost their lives, revel in the fact that you are alive and well. It hit me like a ton of bricks. Out of millions, I am still here and breathing. I still feel the way I do, and that's valid. As it's valid for you to feel however you do. But it's astonishing that I'm still here, that my journey isn't over. I may leave tomorrow or the day after, but to know that I have not gone yet must mean something. That I made it this far.

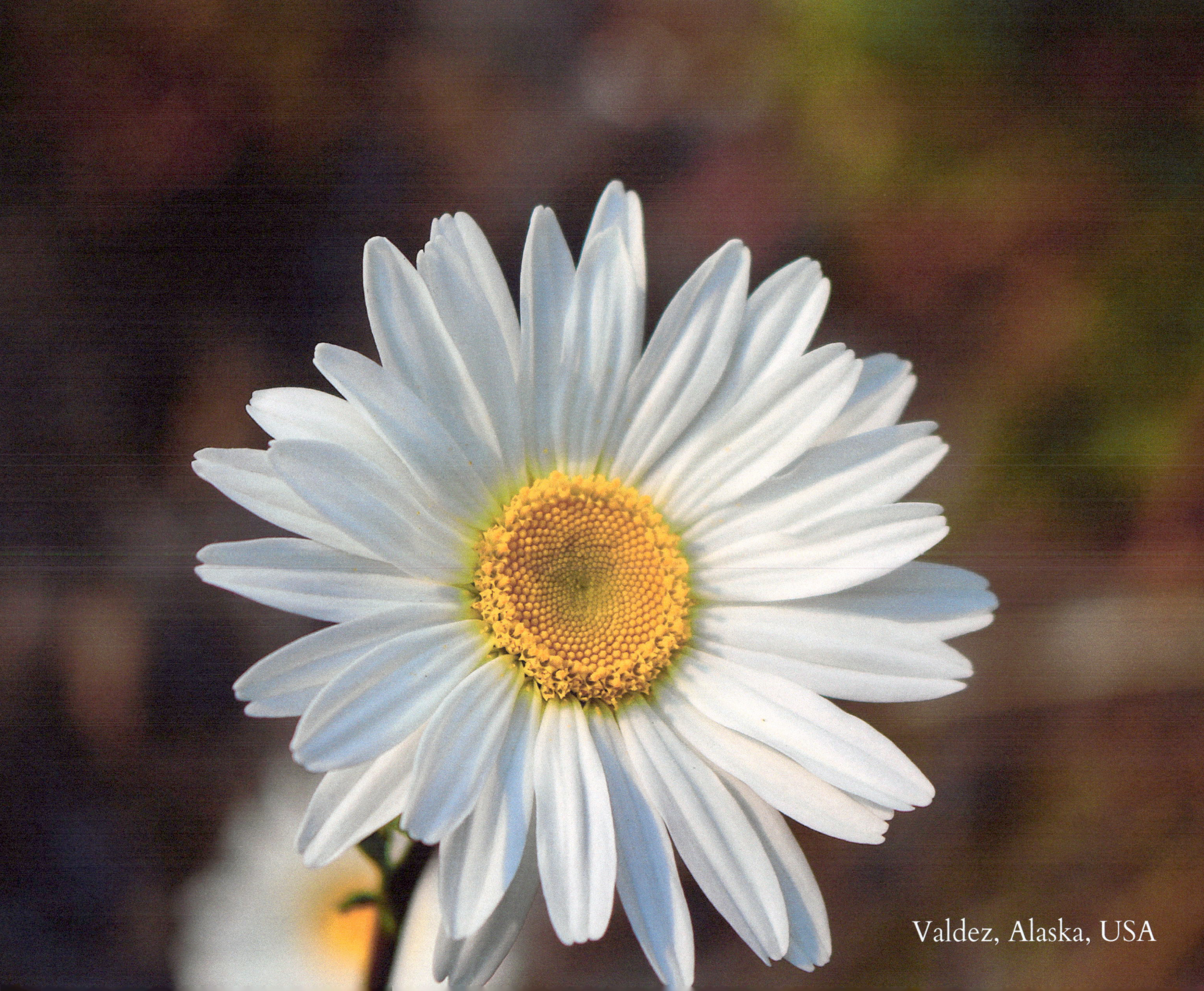

Valdez, Alaska, USA

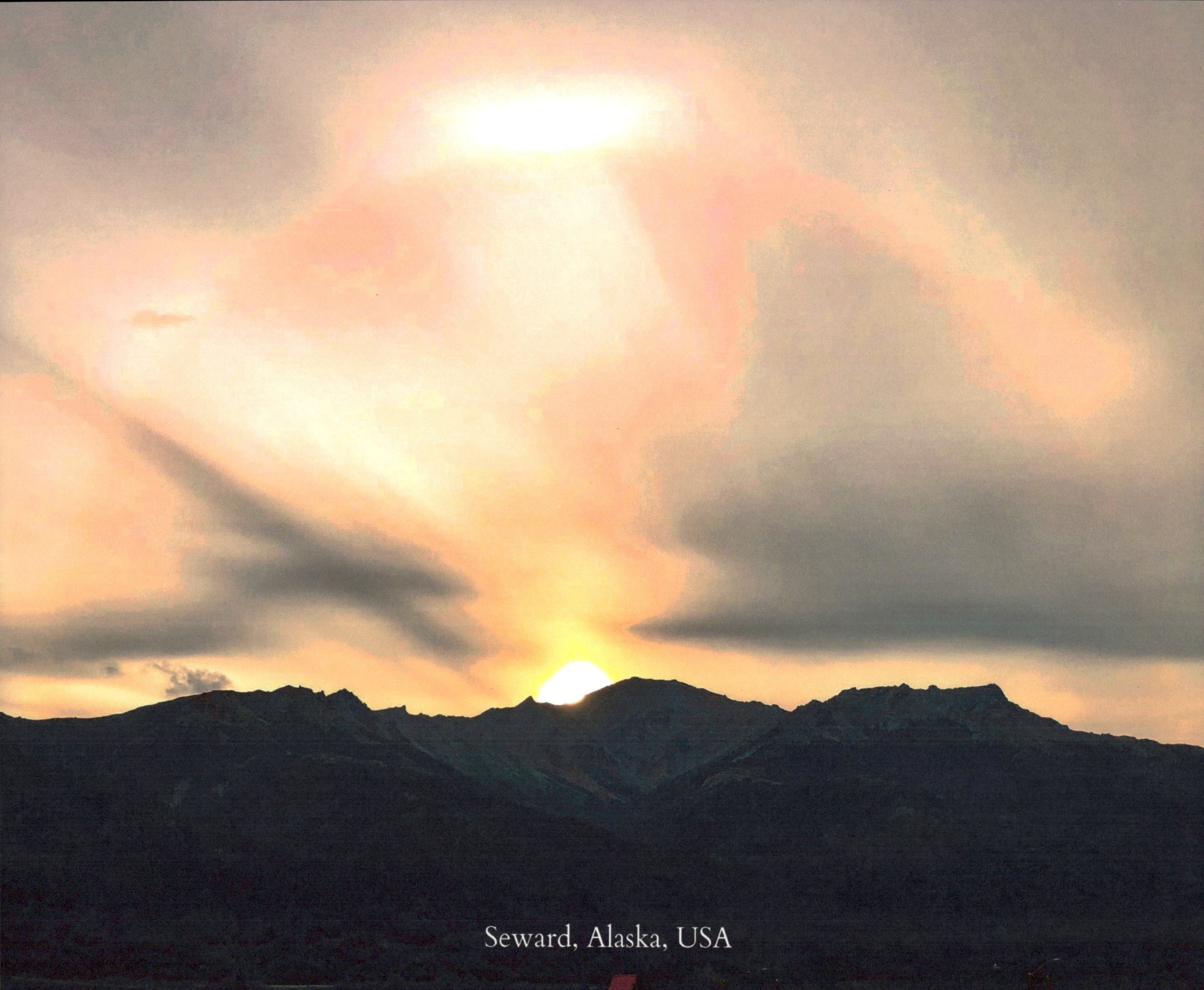

Seward, Alaska, USA

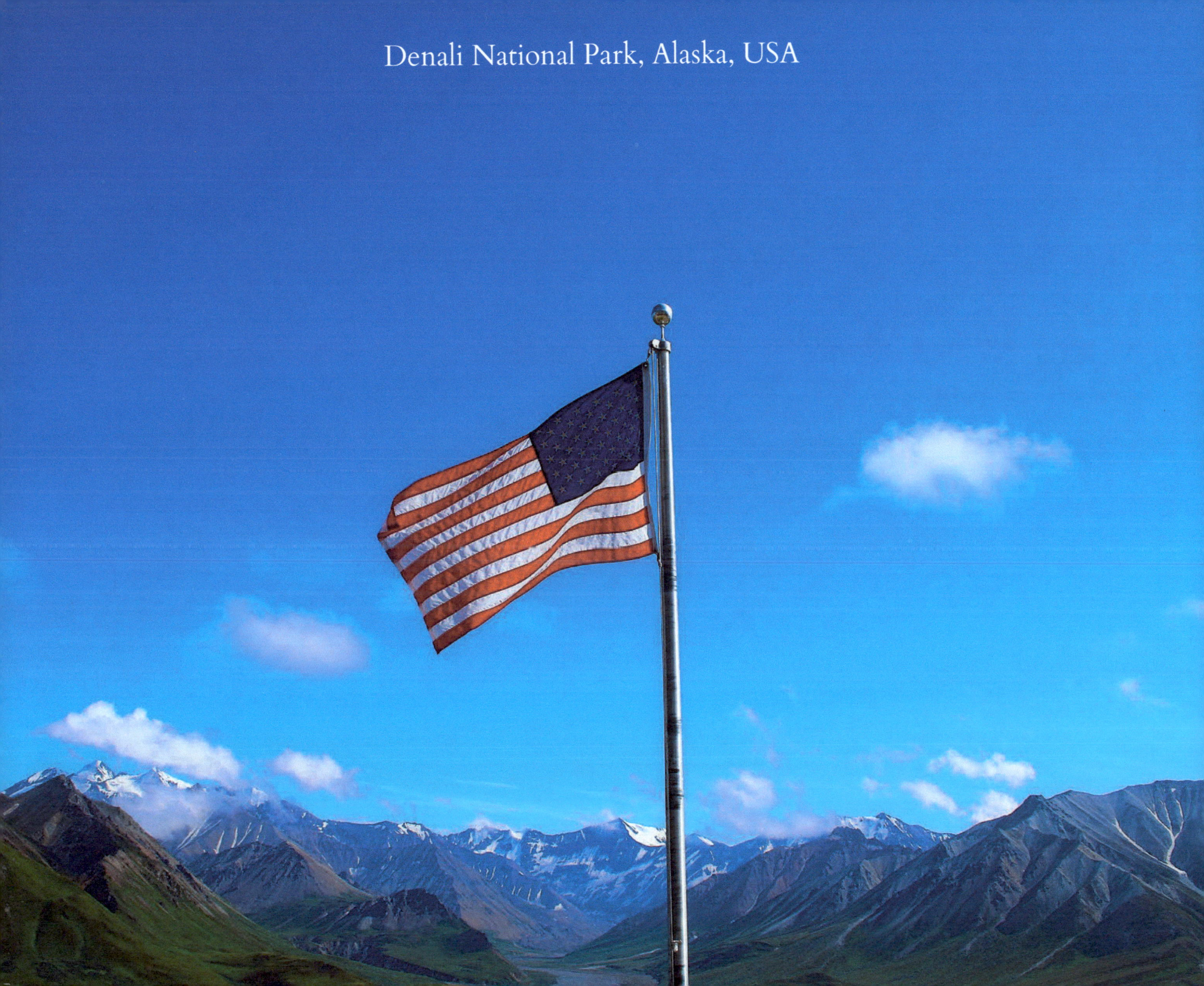

About the Author

Iman Zaynab Bajwa is a medical student with a passion for photography and poetry. Born in the US, she moved to the Middle East at an early age and quickly developed an appreciation for different cultures whilst gaining an outlook she would otherwise never have. Now going to medical school in Pakistan, she's learning even more about the differences in culture and tradition that make us all unique and yet, hold humanity together.

This book is an amalgamation of all of this.